To Bev,
in the belief
hope for us
love Richard
x

ECI Ventures meets hundreds of aspiring entrepreneurs every year. They intrigue us with their determination, vision, and abundance of ideas. They frustrate us, amuse us, but above all we recognize that these are the people that make the difference. These are the 'warriors' of our time.

We asked Tom Lloyd to write *Entrepreneur!* because he shares our curiosity and has been studying this special breed for many years. We believe *Entrepreneur!* provides a new insight and captures the special spirit of these people.

# ENTREPRENEUR!

## THE eci GUIDE
VENTURES

### TOM LLOYD

BLOOMSBURY

ECI Ventures,
Brettenham House,
Lancaster Place,
London WC2E 7EN.
Telephone: 071–240 5050

First published 1992
by Bloomsbury Publishing Limited, 2 Soho Square, London W1V 5DE

Copyright © 1992 Tom Lloyd

The moral right of the author has been asserted

British Library Cataloguing in Publication Data

A CIP catalogue record for this book
is available from the British Library

ISBN 0 7475 1142 X

10 9 8 7 6 5 4 3 2 1

Photoset by Parker Typesetting Service, Leicester
Printed in England by Clays Ltd, St Ives plc

# CONTENTS

To Tony Lorenz
(1944–1990)
Formerly Managing Partner
of ECI Ventures

# Preface

This book is based on conversations with eight entrepreneurs, to all of whom I am extremely grateful.

They are, in the order in which I talked to them:

- Chris Curry, co-founder of Acorn Computers and inventor of the Keyline teleshopping system.
- Martin Sorrell, architect of WPP, the world's largest marketing services group.
- Richard Noble, holder of the World Land Speed Record and one-time aircraft builder.
- Brian McGowan, co-founder of Williams Holdings, one of Britain's largest industrial holding companies.
- Keith Duckworth, founder of Cosworth, the world's leading manufacturer of high-performance car engines.
- Bob Payton, founder of My Kinda Holdings and hotelier and restaurateur extraordinary.
- Andreas Whittam Smith, founder of the *Independent* newspaper.
- Jenny Pitman, Britain's leading National Hunt racehorse trainer.

I have also received much help and advice from Ian Salkeld and

Entrepreneur!

Jonathan Baker of ECI, sponsors of this book, and from Kathy
Rooney, my editor at Bloomsbury.

My thanks also to Hugh Thompson for his support and
interest in the project, and to Sheila O'Connor, who first suggested two of the entrepreneurs.

I also owe a debt to several other authors, particularly to Paul
Burns and Tony Kippenberger (*Entrepreneur*, Macmillan,
1988); Jenny Pitman and Sue Gibson (*Glorious Uncertainty*,
Collins, 1984); Graham Robson (*Cosworth*, Patrick Stephens,
1990); Anita Roddick and Russell Miller (*Body and Soul*,
Ebury Press, 1991); L.T.C. Rolt (*Isambard Kingdom Brunel*,
Longman Green, 1957); Michael Crozier (*The Making of the
'Independent'*, Gordon Fraser, 1988); and Mick Brown
(*Richard Branson − The Inside Story*, Michael Joseph, 1988).

Other sources include newspaper and magazine articles,
radio interviews, published research and my own book, *Dino-
saur & Co.* (Routledge, 1984).

# Introduction

Tony Lorenz, to whom this book is dedicated, used to have a sign on his desk that read, 'The road to success is always under construction.' It was an appropriate sentiment for a man who had transformed Equity Capital for Industry from a creature of government industrial policy into a mainstream venture fund management company.

It was also an appropriate sentiment for a venture capitalist because the men and women in that line of work constitute one of only two groups of business people who delight in journeying along roads that are under construction.

This book is about the other group, those with whom venture capitalists travel along those unmade and often unmapped business roads – the entrepreneurs.

The English word 'entrepreneur' comes from the French verb *entreprendre*, meaning to undertake. I can't help wondering how much discussion about the meaning of the word might have been avoided had the language used in the environment within which entrepreneurs first emerged in any number not already reserved the literal translation of the French noun for more morbid semantic purposes.

*The Oxford English Dictionary* defines an entrepreneur as 'a. The director or manager of a public musical institution. b. One who gets up entertainments. **c. Pol. Econ.** A contractor acting as intermediary between capital and labour, 1885.' The first two meanings have fallen into disuse now, and the third smacks too much, in the 1990s, of the sterile jargon of nineteenth-century political theorists.

It is interesting to note that the first major account of the entrepreneurial phenomenon, *The Lives of the Engineers* by Samuel Smiles, appeared in 1862, two decades before the *OED* lexicographers date the origin of the word's modern meaning.

In those days, when memories of the Great Exhibition of 1851 at Crystal Palace were still fresh and when the modern world was manifestly British, and only recently built by the great railway pioneers, Stephenson, Locke and Brunel, the meaning of the word 'engineer' was more or less equivalent to the modern meaning of 'entrepreneur'.

One must not generalize too much about entrepreneurs. It is too easy to see them as a race apart – a particular mutation. They come in all shapes and sizes. There is little that is standard about them, apart from the entrepreneurial things they do. Those, too, take many forms, and come at different stages of an individual's life.

Entrepreneurialism (such a clumsy word) is like greatness – some are born with it, some discover it and some have it thrust upon them.

Whatever the origins of this quality, it is clearly an economic phenomenon of major importance. It is one of a number of business qualities that violate the first law of accountancy, which states that 'if you cannot measure it, it can't be all that important'.

Nothing, of course, could be further from the truth. Just as evolution in the animal world is driven by the accumulation of small differences, so the imperceptible and unmeasurable features that distinguish entrepreneurs from ordinary people together constitute the engine that drives the evolution of industries and brings about what we call 'progress'.

The American economist Israel Kirzner has tried to integrate a quality he calls 'entrepreneurial alertness' into economic theory and has argued that although it is hard to measure or make a market in, it ranks as a fourth factor of production, equivalent in importance and in scarcity to land, labour and capital. According to this view, 'entrepreneurial alertness' becomes an aspect of cultural vision – an optical sensor system that constantly scans the business environment for opportunities or, as Kirzner says, for 'concatenations of events, realized or prospective, which offer pure gain'.

Tom Peters, the US management guru, puts the point in a style that conveys more of the strangeness of this way of seeing. He says entrepreneurship is 'unreasonable conviction, based on inadequate evidence'.

If one can say anything about what quality distinguishes entrepreneurs, it would have to be something to do with their vision. Everyone knows the odd feeling of suddenly seeing something or someone perfectly familiar in a totally different way. It could be a building, an everyday object, a word, or even a friend. It is as if, just for a moment, a quality that was previously hidden breaks through the habitual way of seeing and presents itself as fresh and strange.

The vision systems of entrepreneurs are wired that way. They see things, in objects and situations, that lie hidden below the threshold of normal awareness. Their minds are more open and more inclined to see the positive side. This generally positive outlook, which assumes the marginal event or encounter is more likely to turn out well than badly, is another quality common to entrepreneurs. As I have observed elsewhere, 'there is no such person as a successful pessimist'.

Where others see problems and difficulties, entrepreneurs see opportunities and possibilities. They turn things, and twist them, until they see a side to them that triggers an idea. They cannot take things for granted, and they have a love for change that borders on the obsessive.

But though an alertness of vision and a basic optimism are necessary qualities in an entrepreneur, they are not enough. As Tony Lorenz knew as well as anyone, good ideas and a fine enthusiasm must be accompanied by daring and determination if the project is to succeed. Venture capitalists are in the business of picking winners.

The quality of being a winner consists of all these elements — a questioning vision, an enthusiasm that makes light of obstacles and set-backs, an appetite for risk and a determination to succeed — manifest in an enormous capacity for work.

Numerous books have already been written about the journeys of entrepreneurs from frustration and obscurity to fame and fortune. They are stirring tales, full of adventure and romance. They tell of the triumphs of Davids over Goliaths, and of the will and dogged optimism that conquer scepticism and the inexorable workings of Murphy's Law. However, few of these books tell much about the entrepreneur as a human being living in the ordinary world, among people with more prosaic business visions and loved by those who can see a little of what entrepreneurs are like, but can never quite come to terms with their passionate craving for independence and their insatiable appetites for novelty and risk.

This book tries to make good this lack. It is based on long talks with entrepreneurs who have operated with more or less success in a wide variety of business areas. Some of them are better known than others, but they all share the qualities that add up to 'entrepreneur' and, in their very different ways, they have all refused to take their world as they found it.

I hope that the range of subjects I have chosen, from the holder of the World Land Speed Record to a leading National Hunt trainer, demonstrates the variety and the ubiquitousness of the qualities we call entrepreneurial. To my mind entrepreneurs are the creators not only of conventional businesses, but of almost every aspect of our world.

And they keep on creating, in foul economic weather as well as fair. There is no rest for the entrepreneurial spirit. It is in a state of constant activity which, if anything, intensifies during recessions, as companies and careers break up and more people are thrown back on to their own resources and initiative. It is often forgotten that the company birth rate, as well as the company death rate, rises sharply in a recession.

Despite the impression sometimes given by the media, and by the honours system too, there is nothing 'fashionable' about the spirit of enterprise. It is an economic fixture that, in the English-speaking world, anyway, and increasingly now in continental Europe, is backed by a large, dedicated source of capital.

British entrepreneurs are always moaning about the myopia of venture capitalists who declined to back them, but in their heart of hearts most of them know that in the 1980s people like Tony Lorenz began to make the world a less hostile place for those with the vision and the determination to succeed.

# CHAPTER 1
# Early life

# CHAPTER 1

# Early life

There are various theories about what features of early life fix the entrepreneurial character, but most suffer from the weakness of being rationalizations after the event.

We discover, during our research, that a child was neglected by his or her father or mother, and we say, 'Ah, so that was it. The entrepreneurial life was a way of compensating for a lack of approbation and approval during childhood.' Or we find the entrepreneur grew up in grinding poverty and, being able and energetic, was driven by the frustrations of early deprivation to determined self-improvement.

The entrepreneurial life, according to such 20/20 hindsight theories, is stimulated by, and becomes a remedy for, the psychological traumas or material deficiencies of childhood. The entrepreneur is a creature of circumstance, distinguished from others because of nurture rather than nature.

But the psychological complexities of a human being's early life are far too intricate for this sort of analysis to be plausible. Evidence to support practically any psychological theory can be found if the researcher digs deep enough into the past. Occasionally, entrepreneurs collude in such speculations and will recall childhood incidents and anecdotes selectively to corroborate this or that theory. As people grow older, they often acquire a need to make sense of their lives – to craft a personal history that is logical and consistent, and which reveals direction and purpose.

Usually, however, entrepreneurs care little about the origins of the energy that drives them. It is too familiar to be interesting. Being practical people, entrepreneurs tend to take themselves as they are. They are too interested in what is going on around them to wonder about what goes on in their own heads. Their energy is directed outwards; they have no appetite for introspection.

So why is it that even those who repudiate the idea that the developmental and genetic secrets of entrepreneurialism lie in the early lives of entrepreneurs are still fascinated by tales of their youth? Perhaps it has something to do with a widespread admiration for entrepreneurs and a suspicion that, had fate dealt a different hand, one might also have been an entrepreneur oneself. Perhaps by scanning their stories carefully for signs, and for choices they made but which you rejected, you might discover something about yourself.

Although psychological models of entrepreneurialism shed little light on the provenance of this priceless economic commodity, there is a certain amount of evidence to support two common-sense, 'role model' predictions about the origins of entrepreneurs. The Open University's Small Business Research Trust (OUSBRT) found that people are more likely to become entrepreneurs if either of their parents had founded a business or were self-employed, or if they had spent time working for small firms. As we shall see, both of these predispositions are broadly corroborated by the stories of the entrepreneurs in this book.

But whether or not early life and experience sow the seed of a later entrepreneurial awakening, there is no doubt that the areas in which entrepreneurs become active are usually fixed (or 'programmed') in early life.

**Richard Noble**, OBE, current holder of the World Land Speed Record, creator of the ARV Super 2 shoulder-wing monoplane and would-be holder of the 'Blue Riband' Hales Trophy, was also programmed early. Indeed, the memory is etched permanently in Noble's mind.

'My father had taken the family for a drive along the north bank of Loch Ness. We saw John Cobb's water speed record boat on the jetty. That was it. I became obsessed. Cobb was 52 at the time and his boat was jet-powered. It was a beautiful-looking thing. It had a design fault, though, and a few days later it killed him.'

The year was 1952 and Richard Noble was six. He says he has found that 'a lot of people get programmed at six'.

He emerged from what he calls a 'standard military family'. His father was a colonel in the Queen's Own Highlanders and was stationed in places as far afield as Libya and Austria. 'I've no sense of home,' he says, 'no real base.' (The feeling of dislocation was common among military children after the war, as Britain extricated herself from the responsibilities of being a world power.)

It was while his father was stationed at the regimental HQ in Inverness that the fateful encounter with Cobb's speedboat occurred. Afterwards Noble became an addict of everything to do with high speed and record-breaking. He read books about all his heroes and their strange-looking machines, and became very interested in gas turbines. 'I was fascinated by it and, at the same time, a little frightened,' he recalls. 'It was an obsession.'

In 1954 he went to Horris Hill, a boarding prep school near Newbury, where he was a contemporary of, among others, the author and of Max Hastings, editor of the *Daily Telegraph*. He did not like it much because it wasn't technical enough.

His main interest at the time was model planes. Like many of his contemporaries, he was an avid reader of the annual Gamages' toy catalogue, especially the section on model aero-engines, a subject on which he was an acknowledged expert.

Noble did not distinguish himself in the classroom or on the field. 'I wasn't a team person,' he says. 'More a guerrilla; a loner.' But he passed the stiffest of public school entrance exams into Winchester, his father's Alma Mater. Here things were better. There were exciting activities such as flying, there were many interesting people and there was a reasonable engineering shop. Looking back, Noble thinks an even better engineering shop could have made a difference to his career.

His relationship with his parents was 'full of challenges'. He remembers pleading with his father to let him learn the electric guitar. 'He refused,' Noble recalls, 'so we made our own electric instruments and taught ourselves.' It was an early demonstration of his skill at 'getting round the system'.

But the main bone of contention was his father's love affair with the army, and his wish for his eldest son to take a short-service commission. Noble remembers that there was a very clear distinction between the military and commercial areas at the time. 'My father wanted me to go into the army but I hated the idea. It was a totally structured environment. The major wars were over, and it seemed to me the army was, and would probably remain, remote from ordinary civilization.'

Although, as revealed later, the army was to give him one valuable experience, Noble successfully resisted the paternal pressure to join up. He obtained A Levels in maths, physics and chemistry, decided to 'duck' university – 'There didn't seem to be any point. I didn't know what I was going to do.' – and joined ICI's paints and wallpapers division. He says this first job was a 'good sales background', but he found it boring. 'The problem was, the organization was not going anywhere.' His appetites for challenge and excitement were beginning to shape Noble's future.

In the case of **Jenny Pitman**, one of the UK's most successful National Hunt trainers, most of the determining factors in her entrepreneurship were established before she was born, when her parents, George and Mary Harvey, leased a 60-acre dairy farm near the Leicestershire village of Hoby. The programming was effectively completed at 14 months when Jenny was given her first pony, Timmy. After that, the chances of her life developing into areas where horses were unimportant became remote.

They became remoter still as she grew up, the fourth of seven

Harvey children. Her initial delight with Timmy soon blossomed into what was to be a lifetime love affair with horses. The
farm was full of them. They were her friends, her playmates and
her father's helpers in the task of making a living during the
post-war years.

The Harvey children used to earn a little extra money for the
family by helping to break in and train the many ponies that
were sent to their father by owners. Jenny was fearless and
loved the work. Perhaps this too — the idea that the Harvey
relationship with horses was more intimate and understanding
than that of other families — was part of the programming.

Jenny was a member of the pony club but she did not go to
camps because the family had no horse-boxes. The children
used to hack to shows and gymkhanas; they also rode to the
shops and the village school.

'There wasn't much money,' Jenny remembers, 'but there
was a lot of love and a lot of interest. Our parents always had
time for us.' The children helped on the farm too; as Jenny says,
'Seven kids can make a big hole in a day's work.'

She did not like school — first at Hoby, and then at Sarson
Girls' School in Melton Mowbray — because it kept her away
from horses. She excelled at sport, but was an indifferent
student. By the time she was 13, she was regularly playing
truant on Mondays and Fridays to join the Quorn hunt on Dan
Archer, a horse her father had bred.

A horse certified by a master of foxhounds to have done more
than a specified number of days' hunting is eligible to race at
point-to-points. Jenny's next step, therefore, was clear. Dan
Archer would earn his certificate and she would ride him at
point-to-points. She was old enough at 14, but it was then
practically unheard of for a girl to ride in races.

They kept the horse at neighbour Albert Riley's farm and, as
race day approached, Jenny would rise at 7.00, walk to the
Riley farm, muck out Dan Archer's stable and feed him. It was
the first time she had worked seriously with a racehorse.

She did not win the point-to-point, but she did win a bet with
her Uncle Percy that she would compete. She described that £1

7

in her autobiography as 'my first, my one-and-only professional riding fee'.

Soon afterwards, while Dan Archer was being raced regularly at point-to-points by her brother-in-law, she encountered a string of proper racehorses being exercised by stable lads. She thought they looked wonderful and began working at their yard on the weekends.

'From that moment on,' she recalls, 'I knew what I wanted to do with my life. I wanted to ride racehorses.' The day she left school, at the age of 15, she went to work full-time for Chris Taylor, the trainer at Tom Venn's Brooksby Grange racing stables. When Taylor and his wife Sarah left to buy their own yard, at Bishop's Cleeve near Cheltenham, Jenny soon followed. It was there she met a young jockey called Richard Pitman.

One of the earliest memories of **Brian McGowan**, co-creator of Williams Holdings, one of Britain's largest industrial holding companies, was overhearing a conversation between his father and mother when he was about 10.

'I didn't understand it, but I knew it was important. Father was 40 and had been at the same private chemicals firm since he was 15. He was assistant company secretary by then and was very unhappy. Mother asked him why he didn't go off and do something different. He said he couldn't because of his pension.

'I vowed, there and then, that I'd never have to worry about a pension, whatever that was. Eight years later I understood the conversation and promised myself I would be financially independent before I was 40.'

McGowan never had any doubts about what he was going to be. 'In my first year at infants' school the teacher asked us what we wanted to be when we grew up. All the rest said something like engine-driver. I said I wanted to be an accountant. I didn't know what it was – until I was 17, I thought book-keeping was something to do with libraries – but I knew that was what I wanted to be. My teacher was amazed.'

McGowan says he is very similar to his friend and Williams

co-founder Nigel Rudd, except that 'Nigel wants to beat every-one. My motivation was to get what the Americans call "FU" money.'

Both men came from lower middle-class homes where money was in short supply, and both complied with, rather than yielded to, parental pressure to take up careers in accountancy. Rudd's mother was a secretary in an accounting firm and had never seen a poor accountant, whereas McGowan was prodded into accountancy by his father.

'He'd always wanted to be an accountant himself but couldn't because his parents couldn't afford the cost of articles. I suppose I was fulfilling my father's dream.' But he does not regard his father's pressure as unhealthy. 'He was genuinely concerned for my best interests. He just thought if I was an accountant I would do well.'

McGowan went to Isleworth Grammar School, where he was junior house captain and captain of the junior cricket team. He says he was 'quite competitive' and earlier had played soccer for the borough of Heston and Isleworth (now Hounslow). How-ever, school was a non-event for Brian McGowan. 'I gained nothing from school. The big thing was when I got articled.'

He was nearly articled to a small firm in Hounslow, but thanks to a family connection, he joined Edward Moore & Sons in the City in the early 1960s.

'It was quite traumatic,' he recalls. 'All the other articled clerks were sons of the clients. I was the first non-public school boy they had articled, and boys of 17 or 18 can be desperately unkind. It stretched me a bit. I watched it for a year and then decided I'd better become just like them. I arrived as a grammar school boy and by the time I qualified, I could have passed for a minor public school boy.'

McGowan never seriously thought of attending university. He was determined to be a chartered accountant, which would take three years if he had a degree and five years if he hadn't. There seemed to be no point in studying for an extra year. He qualified in 1967 at the age of 22 and stayed with Moores for another six months.

An early task was to do number-crunching for an acquisition by the London & Northern industrial holding company. L&N, run by the colourful Jock Mackenzie, was probably Moore's largest client, and certainly its most profitable. The company secretary was impressed by McGowan's work and offered him a job as his assistant. McGowan accepted with alacrity.

It was an important move. L&N was an early example of a new type of company, and had developed a kind of organizational structure that was to become increasingly fashionable in the decades ahead.

'At the centre there was Jock, my boss, me and three girls. It was very decentralized. Profits were £600,000 pre-tax in the year to March 1968 – a lot of money in those days.'

**Keith Duckworth**, designer of the most successful racing engine the world has ever seen, and the co-founder and prime mover of the most lustrous jewel in the British engineering industry's crown, was also conditioned early.

Born in 1933 in Blackburn, the second of two sons, Keith was soon infected by his father's interest in things mechanical. Frank Duckworth was a keen woodworker and loved tinkering with cars. He had a passion for Rileys, of which the family had a succession, and when he was younger he had bought and sold motor cycles.

Perhaps just as important was the environment of commercial diligence and prosperity within which the Duckworth boys grew up. Frank Duckworth was the owner of a weaving shed, and also sold cloth on the Manchester Cotton Exchange. By the time Keith was born, his father's company, Oak Street Manufacturing, was making good profits from weaving and from trading on the Exchange. When he died in 1944, Frank left his family comfortably off in a modest house in Wilpshire, just north of Blackburn.

Keith's mother was the daughter of a blacksmith and was also a formidable personality. Having taken a diploma in domestic science, she became the first female demonstrator of cookers in the Blackburn electricity showroom and raced a motor cycle and side-car on Southport Sands. There was little diminution of the vigorous and independent parental role model for her boys after her husband's early death.

Duckworth remembers being interested in mechanical things at an early age. By the time he was 10, he was mending electric sewing machines and other domestic appliances. 'I was fairly fearless about pulling things apart. Though my father was interested in cars and motor cycles, he had no training in engineering.'

Duckworth's schooling was local and conventional: first, a small private school in Blackburn and then, from 1942, Giggleswick school, preparatory and grammar. He boarded until 1950, played rugger (he was hooker for the First XV), but developed a strong aversion to cricket. He remembers school being a 'very rigorous environment'. He was a rebel and was caned regularly. 'I had little respect for rules. I got into trouble for being out of bounds, in the woods, or bird-nesting in the quarry – for dangerous, boyish things.'

He was also punished for work that was considered poor in relation to his abilities, but he buckled down in the end, taking A Levels in maths, physics and chemistry. He also matriculated, after some extra Latin tuition, to be eligible for Cambridge. 'There was no particular point at which I pulled my finger out. At school there was no option but to work. I ended up as head of house, but I wasn't really suitable.'

However, his overall verdict on school was that it was 'okay – quite reasonable'.

Early evidence of Duckworth's lack of respect for rules, and his inability to take things for granted, both of which would become such striking features of his genius, occurred when the time came for Confirmation. 'Everyone got confirmed,' he recalls, 'but I refused. I do think that was important because it was quite a lot of hassle. I felt it would be hypocritical. I thought very hard about it and I decided I couldn't say the creed.'

He spent his school holidays model-making. He built a radio control system from a design in *Aeromodeller* and he once won a bet with his uncle that he could switch on an electric blanket with radio control from two miles away. He designed his own free-flight model aeroplane – 'It wasn't brilliant, but it flew' – and taught himself metal-working skills in a workshop other enthusiasts of his age could only dream of. This was his father's greatest legacy to him. Shortly before he died, Frank Duckworth had bought a lathe, a drill and a grinder, and had set up a small workshop in the old air-raid shelter at the back of the house. This was where Duckworth had his engineering apprenticeship. 'I learned things there I didn't get at university,' he says. How many more great engineers might Britain have produced if there had been more fathers like Frank Duckworth?

Inspired partly by his interest in model aircraft and partly by an appetite for dangerous pursuits, Duckworth had by now developed his lifetime interest in flying. He decided to apply early for National Service and see whether he could learn to fly with the RAF. On his eighteenth birthday he was in, and learning to fly Tiger Moths.

He thoroughly enjoyed National Service. He says that after school the discipline and the food were easy to digest. However, he was flung out of flight school, just 10 hours away from getting his wings, because of 'dangerous and incompetent flying' – he had fallen asleep. On the other hand, he was top of the course in navigation, and with this success behind him he went up to Imperial College, London, to do a degree in mechanical engineering.

University seemed a natural step. 'If you did A Levels you went to university. I thought if I wanted to be an engineer I had to go. Apprenticeship didn't seem to be an option.' He cannot remember who told him that if he wanted to become an engineer he shouldn't go to Cambridge, but he doubts whether it would have made much difference.

'I've always worked for myself,' says **Bob Payton**, founder, guiding spirit and controlling shareholder of My Kinda Holdings, the holding company for his My Kinda Town restaurants. 'I had a paper round when I was nine, and when I was 14 I was a cabana boy on Miami Beach.'

Payton is a classic entrepreneur. He would probably have made it anywhere, but although he was born in New York state in 1944, grew up in Miami and regards Chicago as his spiritual home, he chose to work his special magic as a restaurateur in England.

After graduating from Miami Beach Senior High School in 1962, he went to the University of North Carolina to do a degree in business. He loved the times — the rock and roll and the ambience, though not the college fraternity system, which he studiously avoided. His father was a far from wealthy travelling salesman, so Payton, like many other Americans (some say that is significant), had to pay his own way through college. One source of money was drumming. 'I played in college bands and I was usually the leader,' he recalls.

Though Payton claims he never really wanted to be the boss 'in terms of running things', he disliked being bossed. He was a reluctant leader, therefore, repelled by the thought of being 'a minion' much more than attracted by the idea of being in charge. This is not an uncommon feeling among entrepreneurs, and it can make them very difficult employees, especially in areas like advertising, where there is just as great a premium on sycophancy in account management as there is on creativity in copy-writing and the art department.

In 1966 Payton went to Northwestern University in Chicago to take a master's degree in advertising. He was in heaven. He was never drafted, but he joined the Reserves and spent a while as a second lieutenant in the US Navy.

After graduating from Northwestern in 1967, Payton joined J. Walter Thompson's Chicago office, where he worked for six years as an account manager. He says he always wanted to be a copy-writer, but he liked the advertising business, even so, because he liked selling people things. It appealed to the salesman in him (perhaps his father's legacy). The main difficulty was that he didn't like it when clients complained when he thought they had no cause to — he wanted to tell them to get lost.

**Entrepreneur!**

Oh, and one other thing about Payton's six years in Chicago, before he was posted to JWT's London office – he acquired a taste, quite an insatiable one, as it happens, for enormous, deep-dish pizzas served by Due's restaurant in the Windy City. There was to be nothing like them in London, for a while...

**Chris Curry**, co-founder of Acorn Computers and the inventor of the Keyline teleshopping system, was programmed somewhat late in life, but did show early signs of an independence of mind.

He was born on 28 January 1946 and grew up in the Cambridge area. He sees himself as very different from his parents. His father farmed in Kenya and then settled down as a farm secretary near Cambridge. Despite the lack of affinity with his kin, Curry got on well with his parents although, until recently, he saw little of his younger brother, who runs a restaurant in Hertfordshire.

His education followed a conventional, middle-class pattern: pre-preparatory school at Cedar House until he was seven (for the last two years he was the only boy in the class), then Kimbolton School in St Neots until the third-year sixth. He was competent at English, French and pure maths but 'pretty bad' at other subjects, and 'hopeless' at sport, apart from being a 'reasonable' cross-country runner. He dreaded the annual humiliation of sports day when parents came to admire their children's prowess, and he also recalls a lot of corporal punishment, of which he seemed to get more than his fair share. But he says that he has strong and fond memories of the school and the masters.

There were three kinds of people at school – swots, goodies and those who 'got into quite a bit of trouble'. He was in the third category. 'I was not a team person,' he says, 'but we formed teams for misdemeanours.' He got on well with the physics master and became a monitor, helping with experiments. He enjoyed that and says, 'Perhaps that was the early stirrings of a technological future.'

Curry liked school. He still goes back there quite often and has kept up with several school friends. None of them are in his business. He obtained A Levels in maths and physics, and flirted for a while with the idea of going to Southampton University. In the event, because he felt an impatience quite common at this stage of the entrepreneurial life, he decided in 1964 to join Pye, the Cambridge electronics group, as a student apprentice. That was Curry's one and only experience of working for a large company. 'I don't fit in with the large corporate environment,' he says. 'I've never done it, apart from Pye.'

After a few months he moved to the Royal Radar Establishment (now the Royal Signals and Radar Establishment) at Malvern, which was, and remains, at the leading edge of technology. It was there Dummer first suggested the integrated circuit, and where Toby and Dinsdale developed the first transistor amplifier. 'It was full of ideas,' Curry recalls. 'People used to come over from America to learn how to make lasers.' He watched the development of the ill-fated TSR2 bomber and worked on super-conducting junctions.

'I left under a bit of a cloud,' he recalls. 'I was supposed to be doing a Dip. Tech. course, but I didn't like it, so I skived.' He says his keen interest in the process of turning inventions into products dates back to that time at Malvern.

Next stop was ITT's W.R. Grace Research Laboratories. Curry says the job was a 'fill-in', but interesting. He helped to develop corrosion test equipment and learned much about the product development process. 'You had to build everything yourself,' he remembers, 'the electronics, plumbing, etc. It was good, practical experience.'

It was while he was at W.R. Grace that he began to notice a brash new name in the electronics hobbyist magazines — that of Clive Sinclair.

**Martin Sorrell,** the architect of WPP, the world's largest marketing services group, was born in 1945, the only child of Jack and Sally Sorrell, and grew up in what he describes as a 'comfortable, North London, Jewish family'.

His mother was a full-time wife and home-maker, and his

father was managing director of the J.M. Stone electrical retailing chain, which he had joined as a salesman straight from school. The company had been split into northern and southern divisions and Sorrell senior ran the latter. With 750 shops, it was the Dixons of its day, and the largest such chain in the UK, incorporating the Civic and Broadmead brand names. It became part of Charles Hayward's industrial conglomerate, Firth Cleveland.

Sorrell remembers Max Stone as the owner of a fierce dog that bit him, rather than as an entrepreneurial role model. He says his father 'wasn't particularly entrepreneurial but was hard-working and very clever'. He was the manager of a division of a public company, a violinist and an amateur Shakespearian actor. When he died in 1989, just after WPP's £527 million acquisition of the Ogilvy Group, Sorrell lost a close friend, a parent but not a role model.

Jules Thorn, founder of Thorn EMI, was a major supplier to J.M. Stone and knew Jack Sorrell well. Martin also met him and was impressed. 'Thorn did have an influence. He was a first generation entrepreneur.'

Bright and athletic, the young Sorrell cruised effortlessly through an education that began at the Goodwin pre-prep school and progressed to Haberdashers' Aske's, where he became captain of the First XI cricket team and of the Second XV rugger team. 'I was an opening batsman, a bit like Boycott; in for hours but never scoring much.' His highest score was 64, and his heroes were the Yorkshire team, where Hutton and Trueman were doing their glorious double-act. He also became interested in football and was a keen follower of Bolton Wanderers.

It seemed inevitable to Sorrell that he should prepare for a career in business. He knew what kind of life it was and he was attracted to it. It was therefore quite natural to go on to Christ's College, Cambridge, to read economics.

An active undergraduate, with 'longish hair', he dabbled in student journalism and was an avid joiner of societies. He was a member of the Labour, Conservative and Liberal clubs because all had interesting speakers. His own politics in those days were 'left of centre'.

After graduating from Cambridge, he went to Harvard, to take an MBA. Sorrell is a great advocate of business schools in general, and of Harvard's in particular. He believes his education provided a very sound base for a career in business. 'Maybe some entrepreneurs would have been even more effective if they'd been through Harvard,' he suggests.

It was an interesting time for a young Englishman to go to Harvard. Sorrell remembers travelling with his friend Simon Schama, now a history professor at Harvard, to Lyndon Johnson's convention in 1964. 'No one cared about the Vietnam War then. It was before the draft. By the time I went to Harvard it had completely changed.'

He was young to be an MBA student – the second youngest in a young Harvard class, and considerably less experienced than the rest. Although there was a good smattering of draft dodgers in his year, Harvard Business School was insulated from most of the youth culture and anti-war protests.

'It was very much a trade school,' Sorrell remembers. 'They weren't the brightest – not as bright as many at Harvard Law School – but people had a sense of direction, and the workload was very intense.'

By the time Sorrell graduated in 1968 Harvard Business School graduates were in such demand that they could command starting salaries of $10,000 a year, virtually twice as much as anyone else going into business.

'You got on the ladder and, sometimes, you never get off,' he says. 'People got sucked into the structure of large firms and became dependent on their high salaries. And at Harvard, we were dealing with the sort of questions you weren't going to have to handle for another 20 years outside.' That is why the most popular occupations for Harvard MBAs of the time were consulting and investment banking. They were seen as ways of getting into businesses at the right level, and of positioning oneself to spot opportunities at client companies.

'That was in my mind,' Sorrell remembers. 'I had no overall

plan, but I was energetic and motivated and I wanted to get involved. I was an opportunist but had a general philosophy about where I wanted to go.'

For his second year Sorrell chose marketing and finance, and also took courses in retailing and in the management of new enterprises. He had decided that marketing was the crucial function because it was about revenue generation. Harvard's emphasis reflected that view – marketing was treated as equivalent to strategy.

The management of new enterprises was a popular course at a time of growing American interest in entrepreneurs and small businesses. It consisted of 40 case studies, only one of which was a failure. Of the 39 successes, one was the high-profile sports management entrepreneur Mark McCormack, who spotted Sorrell's ability. 'He kept in touch,' says Sorrell, 'because he had an idea for starting up in the UK.'

But his first job on graduating from Harvard was with Ralph Glendinning's consultancy at Westport, Connecticut. Sorrell admires Glendinning enormously. 'Ralph invented sales pro-motion games. He was ex-Procter & Gamble, and practically everyone he hired was, too. They used to say he had the P&G phone book.'

When Sorrell joined the Glendinning consultancy division he was the first overseas MBA student they had hired straight from business school. He met some interesting people there, including his first boss Joel Smilow, who now runs Playtex. He also did interesting work for the likes of Heinz, Philip Morris and Pfizer, and was involved in two major acquisition studies, both of which focused on the marketing aspects.

The trouble with consultancy for Sorrell was that 'you never ended up managing anything'. The reputation of Bill Bain's strategic consultancy has been tarnished somewhat in the UK by its association with the Guinness affair, but Bain had the merit, in Sorrell's view, that 'at least it focused on imple-mentation'.

The desire to get closer to the sharp end inspired Sorrell's acceptance of his next two jobs with entrepreneurs, first with

Mark McCormack. He returned to London to help run the UK end of McCormack's burgeoning celebrity management business. He learned a lot from McCormack, but decided the organization was too flat. 'The business was restricted in size because it was concentrated on personal relationships and they were all Mark's.'

While pondering the limited scope for advancement within the McCormack organization, Sorrell bumped into James Gulliver again, a British entrepreneur he had first met at Harvard. Gulliver renewed an offer of employment he had first made in 1968 and this time Sorrell accepted. He became Gulliver's 'personal gofer and financial adviser'.

At that time Gulliver was experiencing a lull in his entrepreneurial career. He had just sold Oriel Foods to RCA, and when Sorrell joined James Gulliver Associates he was in the process of merging his interest in Compton Partners, the quoted London arm of the US advertising agency Compton Communications, with a thrusting young agency called Saatchi & Saatchi.

The complexity of the Compton deal had inspired the brothers Maurice and Charles Saatchi to retain a headhunter to search for a finance director. In their brief they said 'someone a bit like Martin Sorrell would fit our needs'. The headhunter earned his fee by asking whether they had approached Sorrell. They hadn't, so they did.

Of the eight early entrepreneurial lives considered in this chapter, that of **Andreas Whittam Smith**, founder of the only national daily quality newspaper to be launched in the UK this century, contains the fewest clues to his subsequent success.

Whittam Smith himself doubts whether the story of his early life is of any interest. 'There's nothing to say until I started the *Independent*. Someone wanted to write my biography, but I put him off. It would be too short, and of no use to anyone.'

For what it's worth, the biography that never was would have recorded that Whittam Smith was born in June 1937, the son of Cannon J.E. Smith, a vicar in Macclesfield, and that soon afterwards the family moved to a new parish in Birkenhead.

'I grew up in a vicarage in a poor parish and went to the local grammar school. I did very averagely at school. I was not a bad static athlete – the discus and the shot – and I would like to have been a good rugby player, but I wasn't.'

The only incident he remembers as being of any significance in his youth was what happened when his teacher told him he wasn't good enough to go to Oxbridge. 'It was a typical Northern grammar school and sent a lot of people to Oxford and Cambridge. They said to me "We don't think you're good enough," and I found that very annoying.'

He refused to accept the school's judgement. 'I haunted the public libraries and read a lot. I wanted to see if I could go anyway. The scales fell from my eyes. Yes, of course I could. A university is a public institution. Anyone can apply. There was something called a "commonership" for people who failed to get a scholarship. My school was too sniffy about commonerships but I applied and was accepted. I found out Keble College had a clerical background and I thought I could probably get a reference from the bishop through my father.' He applied and was offered a place.

But before Oxford, National Service intervened, and Whittam Smith got annoyed again. 'I failed to become an officer. It was almost automatic for people with my background, but the War Office Selection Board said I was "unfit to lead men". I was very annoyed.'

But in retrospect he has few regrets. He believes his two years in the ranks, square-bashing, was a valuable period. 'I didn't like it – it was like being in a prison for two years with everyone at the bottom of society – but growing up in a vicarage, taking A Levels and then spending two years totally isolated from anyone like me was a great test and I passed it 100 per cent.

'I didn't pretend to be anyone I wasn't and I wasn't treated as anyone I wasn't. It was two years of constant jokes and fun, with never a cross word.' Scum or salt, he liked his fellow squaddies. 'It is easy to forget,' he points out with the objectivity of a fine editor, 'that the same people who are football hooligans at home were very brave soldiers in the Gulf War.'

In mute protest against what he felt was the sheer injustice of the commission board's decision, he made no attempt to rise in the ranks. He was promoted to lance-corporal once and was then relieved of his stripe for not being good at it. 'I accepted the demotion with gratitude. If you're going to be at the bottom, you should be right at the bottom.' But he admits that throughout those two years he felt, 'I'm much better than this.'

Whittam Smith was 'overwhelmed' by Oxford. 'I've never been so knocked out,' he recalls. 'I loved it. I was in heaven. I couldn't understand why anyone complained.' Part of it was the abrupt transition from his lowly status in the ranks to membership of the *jeunesse doré* of the age; but there was more to it than that. 'The social divisions were sharper than they are now, and I'd never really been south before.'

He felt surrounded by brilliant minds, rare talents, vivid characters and glittering performances. 'It was a completely different planet. Yes, it was accentuated by the contrast with National Service.' And it must have crossed his mind that this elevation from hell to a heaven called Oxford was the reward for his diligent research in Birkenhead library.

He was disappointed by his degree, but not unduly surprised. 'I didn't do very well — I got a third in PPE. I led a very social life. I enjoyed myself.'

For some reason Whittam Smith cannot explain he had always read the financial pages, 'even though I had no commercial background. Father earned £700 a year, the idea of shares was completely foreign to me, and I'd never been abroad, except during National Service. I don't know why, but I had always found finance interesting.' So he decided he would be something in the City, although it had not yet occurred to him to be a financial journalist.

Employing the wish-fulfilment system he had already used to good effect, he began researching the City in libraries. 'I discovered that at the top of the pile there was something called the Accepting Houses Committee. I wrote to all 17 of its members. Five firms asked me up for an interview and three or four offered me a job. One of them was Rothschilds and since that was the most famous name of all, I accepted.'

So, in December 1960, at the age of 23, Whittam Smith joined N.M. Rothschild as a clerk checking bills of lading for, among other things, shipments of human hair from China. He remembers being told by the doorman that he was replacing Oliver Marriot (later a distinguished financial journalist), an extraordinary character, in the doorman's view, because he was an Old Etonian *and* a socialist.

As many do, he fell into journalism by accident. He had met Richard Clements, then city editor of the *Glasgow Herald*, at a party and was invited to write a column on the City. 'I wrote rubbish to start with. I did it all from cuttings in the FT library. I didn't realize journalists also went to press conferences.'

He had no sense of calling. 'I simply needed a way of making more money. I was earning £700 a year, and I worked out the income I needed to have the social life I wanted was £1,800. It only occurred to me to increase my income, not to reduce my spending.'

From such casual beginnings a distinguished, if peripatetic, journalistic career grew. In 1962 Whittam Smith joined the *Stock Exchange Gazette* (later the *Investors Chronicle*) full time. A year later he moved to the *Financial Times* and the year after that, in 1964, he joined *The Times*. In 1966, at the age of 29, he moved to the *Daily Telegraph* as deputy City editor, and in 1969 he was appointed the first City editor of the *Guardian*. A year later he returned to the re-named *Investors Chronicle* as editor.

In 1977, at the age of 40, he was appointed City editor of the *Daily Telegraph*, where he might have stayed until the end of his working life, with a chance of ending up as editor of the paper, had an entrepreneur called Eddie Shah not intervened.

# Reflections

Early life exerts a profound influence on how a personality develops, but this influence is far from straightforward. Only the case of Keith Duckworth corroborates the simple idea that entrepreneurial parents breed entrepreneurial children. In the other seven cases the children became entrepreneurs despite, rather than because of, the examples set by their parents.

And though the areas in which the entrepreneurs were to make their marks were clear early on in the cases of Pitman, Noble, Duckworth and, to a lesser extent, McGowan and Curry, who could have predicted that, even in their twenties, Sorrell would shine in advertising, Payton would be a restaurateur and Whittam Smith would become a publisher of quality newspapers?

None the less, it is true that the parents of other entrepreneurs seem to have provided positive role models for their children. The parents of Richard Branson, founder of the Virgin group, both set positive examples. Father Ted was a barrister, and thus self-employed, while mother Eve made embroidered cushions and velvet matchbox covers, which she sold to Harrods. Mick Brown's fine biography of Branson depicts his mother as the more powerful influence, instilling in her children a life-view that emphasized independence, motivation, being a self-starter and standing on your own two feet, and which saw shyness as a weakness.

A feature of Branson's entrepreneurial career is how early it began. As a boy he was constantly dreaming up money-making schemes, ranging from growing Christmas trees to breeding budgerigars. His inability to take authority and the establishment for granted was also evident early on.

He was at Stowe at the time 'student power' was getting up a head of steam. While most simply threw in their lot with the student rebels, Branson's instinct was to try to mediate. He wrote a letter to his headmaster, spelling out ways in which the school could be improved. When his overtures were gently rejected, he and his friend, Jonathan Holland-Gems, began plotting a magazine for their house. The idea quickly grew into an inter-school magazine aimed at sixth-formers which would call for the abolition of fagging, corporal punishment and of compulsory attendance at church and school matches. It was to be called *Student* and it gave Branson a sense of purpose for the first time. He was a fearless letter-writer, and successfully solicited messages of support for the magazine from such luminaries as Yehudi Menuhin, Robert Graves, Ted Heath, Bryan Forbes, Peter Sellers and William Rees-Mogg.

He persuaded his father to let him leave Stowe early, when he was only 17, and the first issue of *Student* appeared the following year, in January 1968. When bidding his pupil farewell, Branson's headmaster predicted, with equivocal prescience, that 'you will either go to prison, or become a millionaire'.

Isambard Kingdom Brunel, the great nineteenth-century engineer, may also have been influenced by a positive parental role model. His biographer, L.T.C. Rolt, records that by the time Brunel had reached adolescence, his father Marc 'had already achieved honour and distinction as an engineer, moved freely in good society and was able, despite financial vicissitudes, to give his son an excellent education and training'.

Aided by his son, Sir Marc designed and completed, after numerous set-backs, the first tunnel under the River Thames, between Rotherhithe and Wapping. It forms part of the modern Underground system.

But, Rolt argues, 'such advantages alone cannot make the man'. He says Brunel's name 'would not mean what it does today if he had not displayed the same characteristics of dogged persistence and an unlimited capacity for hard work which distinguish the self-taught engineers, with the addition of gifts which they lacked. For he was more than a painstaking and ingenious craftsman: he was also an artist of remarkable versatility and vivid imagination. But what most distinguished him was the force which drove him, so long as life lasted, to the utmost limit of his bent and which charged his personality with that mysterious magnetic power which so often discomfited his

opponents and which drew lesser men to follow him, sometimes to prosperity but not infrequently to heavy financial loss.'

Another entrepreneur whose career may have been moulded
by enterprising parents is Anita Roddick (née Perella), founder
of the Body Shop. She grew up in a small Italian community in
the south coast resort of Littlehampton. The man she knew as
her stepfather and called 'Uncle Henry', but who was, as she
found out to her delight years after he died, her real father,
showed distinct entrepreneurial qualities. He transformed the
family business, an old-fashioned 'greasy spoon' café, into a
US-style diner, with a bar, high stools, pinball machines and
Littlehampton's first jukebox.

Roddick records in her autobiography that the facelift made
the Perella's old Clifton Café 'the most popular hang-out in
town'. It was her 'first lesson in marketing aesthetics and the
importance of theatre in creating an atmosphere. ... I remember being dazzled by the Americana, by the Vargas girls on the
Coca-Cola promo cards, by the brilliant colours on the jukebox
and the style of everything.'

She was also an adept trader at school. 'Uncle Henry', who
died in 1952 when Anita was 10, had brought a pile of comics
back from a trip to America and she swapped them with the
same Perella skill her mother displayed much later, when she
sold the Clifton Café and used the proceeds to open a successful
nightclub, the El Cubana.

Anita was training to be a teacher by then, but after she won
a scholarship to study in Israel, she soon became hooked on
travelling. Between brief teaching stints, which she always
enjoyed, she travelled widely in Europe and then round the
world, through the Panama Canal to Tahiti and on to Australia, returning by way of Madagascar and South Africa. On
her unexpected arrival in Littlehampton, her mother 'gave a
shriek of joy' and said, 'I've got a wonderful man for you to
meet. He comes into the El Cubana and he's so like Henry it's
unbelievable. I've been showing him all your letters so he can
read about you. His name is Gordon – Gordon Roddick.'

But though Branson, Brunel and Roddick all had enterprising

parents, the evidence for the parental role-model theory is far from conclusive. All that can be said with confidence is that having enterprising parents is no handicap. It helps, but it is neither a necessary nor a sufficient condition for the subsequent blossoming of an entrepreneurial personality.

From these glimpses of early entrepreneurial life it seems to me that the quality common to all the people discussed is a strong sense of personal freedom – a sturdy and instinctive independence of mind and character. Each has demonstrated an adamant refusal to take things for granted and a determination, not always active, but clearly visible from time to time, to take fate into his or her own hands.

It was this that drove Noble and Roddick to travel widely, that inspired Duckworth and Whittam Smith to kick against the pricks of officialdom and established authority, that was revealed in McGowan's reaction to his father's concern about a thing called a pension, that led Sorrell and Curry to move restlessly from job to job, that stimulated Payton to abandon a career in advertising, and that induced Branson and Pitman to break ranks with their peers.

The entrepreneurial spirit has something to do with an individual's general outlook – with how changeable things appear to be. Does the cup of freedom which life contains seem half empty, or half full? Another thing that distinguishes entrepreneurs from other people is that they believe they are living in an adjustable world.

# CHAPTER 2
# The awakening

# CHAPTER 2

# The
# awakening

Despite a lack of any clear evidence that personality traits determine whether or not a person becomes an entrepreneur, I find it hard to believe there aren't some combinations of elements that, when mixed together, would cause Nature to stand up and announce, 'This is an entrepreneur.'

I also find it hard to believe that these critical combinations, whether or not they can ever be identified, are sufficient conditions for the emergence of an entrepreneurial career. I think entrepreneurial potential exists in a much larger proportion of the population than is accounted for by active entrepreneurs, but that it usually remains latent through lack of an appropriate stimulus at an appropriate time.

Quite what 'appropriate' means in each case will, of course, vary, but there must surely be a point at which some threshold is crossed from the non-entrepreneurial to the entrepreneurial life. It may be crossed very early on, as in the case of Branson; it may be approached with deliberation, as in the cases of McGowan and Duckworth; or it may come about unconsciously, in a way that surprises the individual concerned. There are many routes to an entrepreneurial awakening.

And the threshold point itself, sometimes camouflaged and at other times clearly visible to the traveller, will take many forms.

# Entrepreneur!

It may be an abrupt concatenation of events, as economist Israel Kirzner puts it, or a point at which feelings of frustration reach a critical level, or when what began as a daydream is transformed, bit by bit in the mind of the dreamer, into the embryo of a plan.

Pieces of paper often play a crucial role, particularly the backs of envelopes. I know from my own experience the power a piece of paper, or half an hour with a spreadsheet, has to endow a dream with substance and credibility. There is nothing quite like the feeling of running auto-calc (a computer programme) on assumptions that seem at the time to be reasonable, but which are always absurdly optimistic, and seeing a thrilling picture of a viable business being painted by numbers before your eyes. The adrenalin released at such times can carry an aspiring entrepreneur a very long way.

But although entrepreneurs have a much greater appetite for risk than most, they are seldom foolhardy. Crossing the threshold must seem, at the time, to be a reasonable step to take. There must be a background of plausibility to it all — something that makes it more than mere bravado. Role models often provide such background plausibility.

The cases of parental and other early-life role models have already been considered. This chapter examines other kinds of entrepreneurial exemplar that play a role in awakening the entrepreneurial spirit, and sometimes act as providers of background plausibility.

It is, if not a truism, at least a circularity to say that an enterprise culture tends to encourage the emergence of entrepreneurs. If there are lots of entrepreneurs about, there is greater background plausibility for the aspiring entrepreneur than if they are thin on the ground. However, the prevailing economic climate is probably far less powerful than particular experience. Personal contact with one or more entrepreneurs, either through working for them or some other kind of association, humanizes the breed and makes it less exotic.

Nolan Bushnell, founder of Atari, put the point well when he explained the epidemics of entrepreneurialism that raged through Silicon Valley and up Route 128 in the mid-1980s. He pointed out that everyone working in those areas 'knows at least three millionaires they think are stupid'.

Often it is the stupidity, or other perceived weakness, not the brilliance, of entrepreneurs that encourages others to follow them. Nothing is more reassuring for the aspiring entrepreneur than to meet people who have done what he or she is contemplating, and yet who seem flawed and ordinary. No matter that their perceptions may be clouded by ignorance and arrogance, the effect is to provoke the classic question that precedes the awakening: 'If he can do it, why can't I?'

As described in Chapter 1, the first part of **Richard Noble**'s awakening took place when he was six, on the banks of Loch Ness. The sight of the doomed John Cobb's jet-powered speed-boat haunted him for years, waiting for the right blend of experience and opportunity to launch him on his entrepreneurial career.

Shortly before Noble joined ICI to sell paint and wallpaper, his father, still nursing a faint hope that his eldest son would see the light and choose a military career, persuaded him to sign on for an army outward-bound course. On the day he was due to leave, he was offered a job as deckhand on Sir William Kaiser's yacht for a four-month cruise around the Mediterranean. The glamorous invitation was turned down and Noble went on the outward-bound course. He still regards it as one of his best decisions. 'It lasted a month and was very tough. You learn things about yourself when you're 400 feet up a sheer rock face. It was a crucial point for me. It gave me self-confidence and self-esteem and was a worthwhile challenge. I was very proud of making it.'

Selling paint and wallpaper was pretty tame after that, and Noble was soon in search of more adventurous work. He heard that ICI's fibres division had just begun to market Crimplene, a textured polyester yarn made under licence from Dupont. That sounded more like it, so he asked to join. In those days, however, it was difficult to change divisions in ICI. He had to leave

**31**

for a day and then rejoin. It was worth it.

'We started with sales of £9 million and built it up to £80 million in two years. I was responsible for £20 million of that growth and I drove vast distances. My patch was the East End of London, in the old enterprise culture. Everybody was living on the line all the time. I loved it.'

But as is the way with all fashion fabrics, Crimplene's time ran out. The Dupont patent expired, competition flooded in and the pioneering atmosphere faded. Noble lost his appetite for the job and his feet began to itch.

'I was aware I had missed out on travel, so I bought a second-hand Land Rover and advertised for passengers for a trip to Cape Town at £195 all in. I had 160 replies. Sally [now his wife] was the first to sign on. We stayed three months in South Africa looking for passengers to finance the return trip and then went back via India. The round trip was 39,000 miles.

'It was a brilliant group. We each put £50 in the food kitty for living expenses, and when we got back I paid everyone £18. We survived for four months on £32 a head because we lived at the African level. Travel is about people, not places.'

So enthusiastic had he become about such adventures that he tried to set up a company offering challenging holidays. 'We were going to kick off in Algeria,' Noble recalls, 'but then they nationalized tourism.'

He worked at the American Management Association for a time, selling, writing and running courses, but his heart wasn't in it and John Cobb's ghost was growing restless. 'The land speed thing kept on surfacing. It was always there, but it became more insistent. I'd decided the Land Speed Record was better because there was a motor industry to support it. It was always my dream to do it, but I was frightened of it all — of the engineering and the speed.'

He had become increasingly interested in men like John Cobb and the Campbell record-breaking dynasty. 'I studied their approach to life. They were wealthy individuals, effectively pursuing their hobbies, but there was a lot of engineering and marketing involved too.

'I met Leo Villa, who had been mechanic for Sir Malcolm and Sir Donald Campbell. I asked him what they were like. He was highly uncomplimentary. So why did he stay? He said it was the challenge. They created an exciting space for people.'

While still working at the American Management Association, Noble saw a job advertised in the paper for a sales manager at GKN's building products division. He knew 60 per cent of GKN's turnover was with the motor industry, the most promising sponsors of a Land Speed Record attempt, so he applied and was hired. He then began to pursue the Land Speed Record project more seriously.

Perhaps the turning point was when he founded Project Thrust in 1974, with the declared aim of regaining the Land Speed Record for Great Britain. Or maybe the real awakening, when the idea ceased to be just a dream and began to resemble a plan, was when he sold his beloved TR6 sports car and bought an ex-military Rolls-Royce Derwent engine from an obsolete Meteor fighter. It cost £200 − 20 per cent of his provisional budget.

Buying a jet engine and storing it on blocks in his garage was not a conventional act. It provoked interest. 'A lot of people started to help. Gradually, we got the car together − we ran it at RAF St Athan in Wales and then at Brands Hatch, where we got some TV air time.

'We got close to 200 mph at RAF Fairford, but a wheel-bearing broke and the car [christened Thrust 1] pounded itself to junk.' Noble designed and built it himself and admits he had much to learn.

This, too, could be seen as a turning point. Noble had three options. He could abandon the project, he could rebuild Thrust 1, or he could really go for it and build a brand new, professionally designed car.

'Thrust 1 had been built by friendly amateurs. There was no money, so I issued a press release saying: "Wanted − a 650 mph car designer". I also mentioned all the people who'd helped with Thrust 1.' He thought it might make a good story, and a number of editors agreed.

**Entrepreneur!**

This stroke of genius produced pure gold. The press coverage pulled two key people into the project: John Ackroyd, a car designer at Porsche, and Ken Norris, who had been Sir Donald Campbell's designer and became Project Thrust's 'father confessor', as Noble puts it. Ackroyd was appointed technical director of Thrust Cars Ltd and Noble set about the task of raising money from sponsors. The abortive Thrust 1 project had done its work. Though the main tangible asset had ended up on the scrap-heap, it had given Project Thrust a crucial intangible asset — a reputation for being a serious contender.

The year was 1977 and Noble's plan was to go for the record attempt at Bonneville Salt Flats, Utah, in 1981. The funding task was prodigious. Revenue had to treble every year until it reached a plateau of £350,000 a year — about £600,000 in today's money.

A small team of dedicated craftsmen started work on Thrust 2 in May 1978 at Fishbourne on the Isle of Wight. The car was designed by John Ackroyd round a 22-year-old Rolls-Royce Avon engine with reheat. It came from an English Electric Lightning, the first British plane to fly at more than twice the speed of sound. They chose the Isle of Wight because overheads were low and there were some high-grade aircraft skills in the area. 'John did the engineering,' Noble recalls, 'and I did the marketing, PR and driving.'

Thrust 2 ran in skeleton form in 1980, and on 24 September at Greenham Common in Berkshire he bagged the British Land Speed Record at 248.87 mph. 'We converted that credibility into transonic wind-tunnel work contributed by British Aerospace and into buying an uprated version of our Avon engine — the 302 — which gave us 19 per cent more power. This was an unpopular decision at the time since the engine systems had to be reworked and it was considered then that the first engine gave us enough power to achieve the record [it didn't].'

Things were looking serious, and Project Thrust attracted further sponsorship for the attempt on the World Unlimited Flying Start Mile, commonly known as the Land Speed Record, and the main object of Richard Noble's dream. The target was the 622.407 mph record set by the American Gary Gabelich in his rocket car Blue Flame in 1970. On the way, he would have to beat the last British record of 403 mph set by Donald Campbell in the wheel-driven Bluebird in 1964, and Craig Breedlove's 600.601 mph Jet-Powered Class Record set in 1965.

As Noble recounts, the trip to Bonneville in 1981 achieved only one of these intermediate objectives.

'On the first run we were all over the place, but we scraped 500 mph and broke Campbell's record. Then it rained. We'd insured against desert flooding, but the insurers decided to string it out. They claimed we hadn't made a record attempt.

I told them we would be holding a press conference at which we would either announce we were going ahead or that we were abandoning the project because our insurers were refusing to pay up. They paid up. I got a cheque for £75,000.'

Preparations for a return trip in 1982 were going well when disaster struck during trials at Greenham Common on 17 June. 'It was a day when everything went wrong,' Noble groans. 'I missed a visual marker and there was an appalling accident − there was £53,000-worth of damage to car, and £80,000-worth of damage to engine.'

But the project's momentum was considerable by now and the sponsors rallied round. 'They were magic,' says Noble. 'They all felt part of it. The cash sponsors agreed to fund a rebuild and we did it in 12 weeks.' The RAF also emerged from the affair with credit: 'I was negotiating with the MoD to buy another engine when the RAF said they'd like to look at the old one because they'd never seen one so badly damaged. We sent it up to them at a cost of £200. They looked at it and then asked what they should do with it. I said, "Junk it." They said, "Why? We've rebuilt it."'

As soon as they got to Bonneville in 1982, it flooded. 'We had to find somewhere else and chose Black Rock Desert. We got permission, with the help of a petition from villagers, and we'd just got over 600 mph when it rained.'

This time the sponsors had insured and there was money for a third attempt in 1983. The weather had a few more tricks up its sleeve, but it was weary of the game. On a fine, hot and windless day in early October Thrust 2, with Richard Noble at the wheel, thundered across Black Rock Desert, achieving a top speed of 650 mph and an average speed for the measured mile (in both directions) of 633.468 mph. John Cobb's ghost could rest.

'It was a wonderful organization,' muses the holder of the World Land Speed Record. 'If we'd had to rebuild the car on the track, we'd have done it. It was a totally wonderful team – it refused to be beaten.'

Though **Chris Curry** insists that Clive Sinclair 'was never a role model', it is hard to believe that Sinclair had no influence on how Curry's career developed, even if only by unwittingly providing backgound plausibility.

*Practical Wireless* and *Wireless World* were sober, low-key magazines catering for the sober, low-key electronics hobbyist, so it was quite a surprise for avid readers, like Chris Curry, to be confronted in the mid-1960s by garish, full-page advertisements for radios and amplifiers made by Sinclair Radionics. Curry was intrigued and became more so after he had journeyed to the Scout Hall, Comberton – Sinclair's first home – to buy a Sinclair X10 amplifier.

Soon afterwards, Curry saw another advertisement announcing that this strange company was moving to Cambridge and was looking for recruits. He and a W.R. Grace colleague, Lindsay Lloyd, decided to apply and both were hired. 'It looked interesting and fun,' Curry recalls. It also seemed as if it might provide the opportunity Curry wanted to become involved in the process of turning technology into products.

'The excellent thing was that it was very small, and if you had a project, you saw it right through. You did the electronics, designed the box, bought the components and then organized assembly. It was a very broad education and the work was fun.'

Sinclair's products at that time were radio and amplifier kits sold to the hobby market through mail order, but Clive Sinclair is a prodigious inventor and the place was full of his dreams.

Curry remembers working long hours on Sinclair's miniature TV project, winding deflection coils with hair-thin wire. The coils needed 2,500 turns, and at turn 1,500 the wire invariably broke, or you lost count. The prototype of the TV was shown at the 1966 Radio Show but it was many years before it finally reached production.

One day in 1970 Clive Sinclair returned from a trip to the US with a sample of the world's first calculator on a silicon chip, just unveiled by Texas Instruments, and a bundle of papers. He appointed Curry leader of a development project that was to culminate in 1971 with the launch of the world's first working, single-chip calculator. It was called the Sinclair 'Executive' and retailed at £79. It was later honoured with a place in the Museum of Modern Art in New York.

Entry into the calculator market led to a massive expansion of Sinclair's business. A production line was set up at St Ives, outside Cambridge, and a whole family of calculators was developed. However, the integrated Japanese electronics groups, making both chips and calculators, moved in with Liquid Crystal Displays (LCDs) that were more reliable and used less power than Sinclair's Light Emitting Diode (LED) calculators. Sinclair responded by developing the 'Black Watch', which would have been the world's first mass-produced electronic wristwatch had Radionics not been let down badly by its chip supplier.

The delay, and the product's notorious unreliability, caused Sinclair to seek outside funding for his still-cherished TV project. The National Enterprise Board took a controlling stake in Sinclair Radionics in 1974. The partnership proved less than harmonious, however, and two years later Sinclair suggested to Curry that they set up a separate company to be called Science of Cambridge.

SoC, run initially as a one-man band by Curry, was instantly successful. Its first product was a wrist calculator sold in kit form by mail order for £9. It generated sales of over £150,000 and was highly profitable. Sinclair and Curry were toying with the idea of making a reflecting telescope as a follow-up, when

Curry saw an advertisement in a US hobbyist magazine for a 'computer in a book'. This led, in spring 1976, to the launch of SoC's MK14 kit computer. It employed a calculator display and sold, again through mail order and in large numbers, for £39.95.

It was during the incubation of the MK14 that Curry began to see quite a bit of Hermann Hauser, a Cambridge post-graduate who was studying physics. Curry had befriended the young Austrian a few years earlier when Hauser visited Cambridge to learn English. Now, with the Sinclair role model providing background plausibility, they discussed all sorts of ideas for new business ventures, including the invention and marketing of a new board game.

The MK14 provoked enquiries from companies keen to explore the new technology. Sinclair was not interested in following them up, so in 1978 Curry and Hauser formed CPU Ltd. It was a pun. The initials normally stand for a computer's Central Processing Unit, but in this case they stood for Cambridge Processing Unit. CPU's first project was for a Welsh fruit-machine manufacturer and was worth £3,000.

Curry stayed at SoC for another six months, but left when Sinclair decided to give the MK14 follow-up project to the NEB-backed Radionics. Within months, and with the help and inspiration of some of Hauser's university friends, CPU had given birth to Acorn Computers and was poised to enter the embryonic kit computer market with a state-of-the-art device called System 1 – Eurocard modular computer system.

Then came the Acorn Atom, a single board computer launched almost at the same time as Sinclair's ZX80, to be followed by a contract to design and build a computer for the BBC. Acorn's growth was meteoric. Turnover soared from £31,000 in 1979 to over £93 million in the year to July 1984, the first full year after Acorn's flotation on the stock market with a price tag of £135 million. But nemesis lay just around the corner.

Acorn's cheaper version of the BBC Micro, the Electron, had been launched a year previously but had just missed the crucial Christmas selling season. By the time Christmas 1984 came round, Amstrad had entered the market and Sinclair had cut the price of his Spectrum very aggressively. It was a bad Christmas by the standards of earlier years and the market took fright. In January 1985 Acorn's shares fell to 43p, compared to a peak of 190p, and the share quote was 'suspended' – a sure sign of serious problems – on 6 February at 28p. A fortnight later it was disclosed that Acorn had lost £11 million in the second half of 1984 and that Olivetti, the Italian office equipment group, was to take a 49 per cent interest in the group, reducing the founders' holdings from 86 per cent to 37 per cent.

Though **Martin Sorrell** was clearly influenced when choosing an entrepreneurial career by such examplars as Ralph Glendinning, Joel Smilow, Mark McCormack and James Gulliver, he encountered his most powerful role models at the time he found his area – when he joined Saatchi & Saatchi in 1977.

He loved advertising. 'It's new. It was only really formed in the UK in 1955, when commercial TV started. It was innovative, fast-growing and unstructured, and it is still in the business of creating precedents rather than following them. I found it very interesting.'

But for all its youth, the industry had established a number of conventions by the time Sorrell became an adman. The most important of them was that you did not try to poach clients from other agencies. Charles and Maurice Saatchi had the courage to break that rule and Sorrell admired them for it.

'They were also much younger than the people running the big American agencies,' he points out, 'and in this business you are only as good as your last advertisement. It's a business for high achievers. There's instant feedback.'

It is also a business which has lacked the inclination, and the time, as it has grown, to organize itself into a series of distinct managerial strata. As Sorrell put it, 'You don't have to wade through layers of hierarchy.' A quality he particularly liked at Saatchi & Saatchi was the informality. 'This was very different. Most UK agencies were stuffy, staid and risk-averse. It was really no more than a colony industry belonging to the big US agencies. It wasn't like that at Saatchis. There was no structure and no Buggins' turn.' Talent was valued, achievement was recognized and there were no restrictions. As Maurice Saatchi once said, 'We're in the coup business.'

In Sorrell's view, informality is essential in a fast-moving industry like advertising. At Saatchis decisions were made very quickly during corridor conversations. Sorrell says, 'A bad decision on Monday is often better than a good decision on Friday. Time is crucial and it's becoming increasingly so everywhere now.'

All this meant that there were fewer barriers to advancement in advertising than elsewhere, and this suited Sorrell. When a talented and ambitious individual wants to get on, he or she would do well to choose a field where the barriers to quick advancement, whether in the form of bureaucracy or automatic promotion systems, are relatively low. Sorrell believes that that's why so many blacks and members of other minority groups go into sport and entertainment. It is not that they are unable to succeed elsewhere; it is that in areas where talent is everything, no one can afford the prejudices that restrain progress and require even the most talented of youth to wait its turn.

Sorrell's achievements at Saatchi & Saatchi have never been fully documented, but he is widely credited with three major contributions to the group's phenomenal growth in the 1980s. First, and most important, he was instrumental in persuading the City of the virtues of global advertising. This was no easy task because the City is conservative. Before Saatchi & Saatchi arrived in its midst through the reverse takeover of Compton Partners in 1977, it saw advertising as altogether too arty and fly-by-night to be of much interest to serious investors. But persuaded the City had to be before the Saatchis could win the premium share rating they needed to embark on their stunningly ambitious international acquisition programme.

The speed and success of this extraordinary expansion, which was to make Saatchi & Saatchi the largest advertising group in the world by 1986, is also credited to Sorrell. It began modestly with three minor UK acquisitions in 1978, 1979 and 1981, and then moved up a gear in 1982 with the $55 million purchase of Compton Communications, the former US parent of Compton Partners. This was the first major deal in which Sorrell used the so-called 'earn-out' — a system of deferred consideration linked to post-acquisition profits. It was a major innovation and was quickly adopted by other acquisition-led marketing services groups.

The 'earn-out' confers two advantages. It helps to keep the top people in the acquired company (at least until the final earn-out payment is due) and provides considerable financial 'leverage', as the Americans call it. In the case of Compton, for example, Saatchi & Saatchi made a $30 million down-payment and undertook to pay more later, up to a maximum of $25 million.

Sorrell's third contribution to the Saatchi & Saatchi 'glory days' was to develop a system of financial controls that was also widely admired and copied. In so doing he brought much-needed discipline to an industry that had previously been notoriously badly managed. He also did it without damaging, unduly, that informal, bureaucracy-free atmosphere in which so-called 'creatives' flourish.

The rise of Saatchi & Saatchi culminated in the high summer of 1986, with the £300 million acquisition of US agency Ted Bates. After that it was all downhill towards the crisis capital reconstruction in early 1990, along a route that I and K.E. Sveiby predicted in *Managing Know-how* (Bloomsbury, 1987).

Sorrell had left by then and begun planning his successful campaign to usurp Saatchi & Saatchi's world crown. 'I was a junior partner at Saatchis,' he explains. 'I'd been doing the same job since 1977. When I told Maurice I was looking for a company, he said he was doing the same and he even suggested one to me.'

Sorrell bought his exit ticket, a significant share stake in Wire & Plastic Products, in 1985, and left Saatchi & Saatchi on 17 March 1986. The move was not prompted by a wish to go it alone. 'You're never on your own. You're dependent on others or others are dependent on you.' He says his decision to quit the group he'd done so much to build and buy a tiny manufacturer of wire baskets was not an awakening, but an 'expression of something that happened a long time ago'. He was 40 and, as he says, '40 is a dangerous age – a sort of male menopause.'

Sorrell suggests Charles Saatchi had his 'awakening' at 18, that Maurice went to the LSE and had his at 23, and that Mark McCormack, Ralph Glendinning and Joel Smilow all slept even longer. He also believes the entrepreneurial quality is probably more widespread than it seems. 'It's always latent,' he says. 'Sometimes it comes out.'

Just before Sorrell's departure, Andreas Whittam Smith, the City editor of the *Daily Telegraph*, approached Saatchi & Saatchi with a request for help with market research for a new quality, daily newspaper. Sorrell suggested that they would comply with the request in return for a slice of the action. 'I don't believe, if we had been open about it, there would have been any serious conflict of interest problems in our swapping our know-how for a stake in the *Independent*. After all, we own 20 per cent of *Survival* (the Anglia TV wildlife series) and no one seems to worry about that.'

For **Brian McGowan**, Jock Mackenzie was a flawed role model – an entrepreneur he could look at and think, 'If he can do it, so can I.'

A year after McGowan joined L&N, Mackenzie bought an earth-moving company in Ripley. Its accountant and company secretary was Nigel Rudd. 'I met him at the Savoy for a boozy lunch to celebrate completion. He was the only sane person there and he felt the same about me. We became firm friends. Our kids are about the same age and our families get on. We began to sit down and talk about things as we watched Jock play the game. We learned City craft from him and we also learned how *not* to run a business.'

McGowan's role model at the time was Jim Slater. 'He was a much-maligned man. His mistake was that he didn't run the businesses. They were all like that — Slater, Pat Matthews, John Bentley, Oliver Jessel — they were great dealers, but none of them ran their businesses. Hanson was different. I have often wondered whether he knew it all along, or whether he got lucky and learned.

'Jock thought if you bought 75 per cent of a business and made the vendor very rich, he'd work just as hard for 25 per cent. That was a major flaw. He also indulged in absurdly expensive wining and dining. We disapproved of that. We're parsimonious by comparison.'

At L&N's annual general meetings at Essex Hall, London, Rudd and McGowan would be told to stand behind a curtain and then start opening champagne bottles as soon as questions began. McGowan remembers, particularly, the completion meeting for L&N's acquisition of the Murphy construction group. 'It was at the Café Royal because we couldn't get into the Savoy. It was a complicated deal and we didn't arrive until 2.00. By 6.00 everyone was legless, and Jock and Murphy were on the verge of a punch-up.'

But though McGowan believes Mackenzie's failings had a more powerful influence, he had his good points, too. 'There was no better man than Jock to do a deal. He charmed people. He could handle all types. I've seen him take rough, illiterate guys and have them eating out of his hand.'

McGowan left L&N in 1974 to run P&O's acquisitions team. He loved it. 'It was Establishment with a capital "E". The P&O name got you in anywhere. Jock didn't have that. I'd always known it was important to be accepted by the Establishment.'

But though McGowan's career was developing at a pace others would have found enviable, he began to doubt whether he would reach his target of being financially independent by the time he was 40. 'I was 29 and earning £19,000, which was a very good salary in 1975. But inflation was 26 per cent and tax was 83 per cent. I needed a £10,000 a year rise just to stand still. I thought this was as rich as I was going to get.'

Then one of McGowan's rivals for the finance director's job

at P&O showed him an advertisement in the *Financial Times* for a job in Hong Kong (where tax and inflation rates were much lower) with the Malaysian conglomerate, Sime Darby. 'I went for the money,' McGowan confesses.

Though Rudd was still at L&N, the two friends met regularly to chew the fat. 'At that stage we were playing the game of being the City's angry young men. We always recognized that you never get rich working for someone else and we both felt each had something the other needed. Neither of us could have done it on our own and we couldn't do it now on our own. We're such different people. I'm neat, precise, organized, but I don't have much flair. Nigel does, but he can go off the rails.'

They decided it was no good trying to develop something new, like Sock Shop, because they lacked the right kind of vision and, anyway, it wouldn't be playing to their strengths. 'We understood acquisitions, how to work the City and how to run businesses.'

McGowan and his family lived in Hong Kong for six years. 'It was a great experience. I was running a group at the sharp end. I put in control systems and disciplines, and managed 3,000 people, all but six of whom were Chinese. But I'd gone as high as I could go in Sime Darby and I needed to move. I loved HK but couldn't find a suitable job there.' More important, his wife, Julia, was threatening to go back to England, even if he didn't.

McGowan visited London regularly throughout his time in the Far East and always had lunch with Rudd. 'By October 1981 it had got to the point when Julia said she was going. I told Nigel, "If we're ever going to do it, now's the time." Nigel said, "Fine." It was 3 October, my birthday. On 30 October Nigel rang me in Hong Kong.' The conversation went as follows:

**Rudd:** I've found just the right vehicle.
**McGowan:** Where is it based?
**Rudd:** South Wales.
**McGowan:** What is it?

**Rudd:** A foundry.

**McGowan:** (with heavy sarcasm) Terrific!

**Rudd:** You haven't heard the best of it yet. It's losing nearly £1 million a year.

'Luck is the most important ingredient' says McGowan. 'We'd done no analysis, but our timing was perfect.'


**Keith Duckworth** went to his first motor-racing meetings with some university friends, including Noel Davis, now head of the shipbuilders VSEL. 'I remember thinking, "That's good stuff",' but he was always a master of understatement and what he really meant was that he found it absolutely thrilling.

In retrospect it seems inevitable that the young undergraduate, with his new-found passion for racing-cars, would gravitate towards a pub yard in Hornsey, north London, where one Colin Chapman was building a company called Lotus.

'I had a little money and mother allowed me to buy a Lotus 6 kit.' A perfectionist like Duckworth had to do it right, so he visited Lotus to choose the parts. 'I got bits from Ford, borrowed a trailer to pick up the kit from Hornsey and assembled the chassis and engine in my first summer vac.'

Duckworth's brief flirtation with the idea of being a racing driver is recounted in Graham Robson's book, *Cosworth: The Search for Power*. It was his third outing. He was hammering through the fast Fordwater kink at Goodwood, where there is a change of surface, when his Lotus bucked and went sideways.

'I remember thinking, "Jesus, you're not with that, not even vaguely with that, are you?". I'm hopeless, my hand/eye coordination is poor. It upsets me.'

He had learned there were people with natural ability, and that he wasn't one of them. But he was a naturally gifted engineer and knew there was a role for him in motor-racing. He went to work for Lotus in his second vacation and met Mike Costin, Chapman's technical director. It was the beginning of motor sport's most famous friendship. (I suppose they could have called their company TinDuck, but they chose the alternative.)

## Entrepreneur!

Duckworth 'just scraped through' his finals in 1957. If the smell of Castrol R racing oil had not already gained a firm hold on his senses, he would, in the normal course of events, have joined a large engineering group as a graduate apprentice. 'The Rolls-Royce people interviewed me,' he remembers. 'They said they didn't offer me a job because they doubted that I was suitable to be a member of a team. I was very shy at the time, so that was remarkably perceptive of them.' He was offered a graduate apprenticeship at Napier, and accepted despite misgivings. 'I thought I'd probably have to start filing blocks of metal for weeks and I didn't need that. I'd filed my blocks at 12.'

Graham Hill was about to leave Lotus to embark on his career as a full-time racing driver and Chapman needed a replacement, so Duckworth went to see him and was offered a job as a gearbox development engineer at a salary of £600 a year. 'I'd worked there during two vacations, and built rear axles and close-ratio gearboxes. I'd also built my own Lotus 6 and it ran. Colin thought I'd be useful.'

He spent 10 months at Lotus, re-engineering a pig of a gearbox, known as the 'queerbox'. He solved the original oiling problem, and then tackled the gear selection system. 'I drew and made a positive stop mechanism and got it working.' He was proud of that and he realized he had skills that Chapman lacked.

'Colin had no idea of limits and fits. He was brilliant at concepts, but bad at detail. I didn't think concepts were that important but maybe that was because I realized mine weren't bad anyway. I've no respect for memory either, but I have a very good one.'

It was during Duckworth's struggles with the queerbox that his friendship with Mike Costin blossomed. 'Mike is a very good, intuitive engineer, unspoiled by too much education. Engineering education based on maths covers 10 per cent of the job and makes no suggestions about how to tackle the other 90 per cent.'

The two men talked of starting their own business.

Duckworth is insistent that there were no grand dreams at that stage.

'We both thought it must be possible to make an interesting living messing about with racing-cars and engines. That was the total objective behind the formation of Cosworth – the *total* objective. Most of us thought Chapman was very bright, but we thought the market was big enough for both of us, and the rest of the opposition didn't look that frightening. We thought it was worth a go.'

Cosworth Engineering Ltd was formed on 30 September 1958, soon after Duckworth ran out of patience with the queer-box. 'I got frustrated in the end. Colin wanted an abortion and I wasn't prepared to do it.'

Costin could not join full-time until 1961 because Chapman kept him to his contract, so the original business consisted of Duckworth and a dynamometer. The workload consisted of freelance engineering on racing Elites and Elvas. The break came in 1959, when racing-car manufacturers like Lotus began preparing for the new Formula Junior, a nursery class of single-seater racing inspired by the Italian, Count 'Johnny' Lurani.

After first tinkering with a Fiat engine, Duckworth decided Cosworth would ride into the FJ battle on Ford's new 105E 1-litre engine. It was a fateful and almost a fatal decision.

Having committed himself to the Ford engine, Duckworth had great trouble getting it to produce a competitive amount of power. The problems boiled down to camshaft design and to a phenomenon known as 'jerk' which, according to the textbook, imposed vexing constraints on the shape of cam profiles.

Duckworth remembers the period, just before Christmas, 1959, as the only time Cosworth nearly went under. 'I'd just been refused a £30 overdraft by my bank manager to pay the phone bill. I thought, "Be like that," but I knew I was going to go broke unless the next cam worked. I really sat down to think, and I also talked to Ben Rood [later a director of Cosworth] who used to make cams. He'd developed ways of making cams without advanced mathematics. He was a naturally talented engineer.

'Cams were designed according to the book. There was quite a good argument for jerk, but I decided the book was wrong — that jerk wasn't a problem and that therefore the problems jerk created didn't exist. I made the A2 cam and it worked.'

Duckworth regards his unilateral repeal of 'the law of jerk' as a formative experience. 'It was a powerful discipline because I didn't want to go broke. That threat sharpened the application of grey matter in a big way. Perhaps we all need great pressure to force us into thinking.'

Though **Jenny Pitman** may not see it that way, her love affair with Richard Pitman was the key event in her business career for two reasons: it took her, as the partner of a jockey, into horse-racing's mainstream and it prompted her to leave Leicestershire and make her home in the heartland of racing, where role models were thick on the ground.

Having admitted to herself that her feelings for Pitman had developed into love, Jenny Harvey agreed to leave the Taylors and follow the young jockey to Lambourn. The magnet for Richard Pitman was Fred Winter, champion jump jockey, winner of two Grand Nationals and hundreds of top-class National Hunt races, who was poised to embark on an equally successful career as a trainer.

Richard asked Winter for a job, was hired and found work for his girl at nearby stables owned by Major Geoffrey Champneys. It was here that Jenny began to develop her craft. Champneys thought highly of his 18-year-old stable girl and allowed her to 'school' as well as ride his horses, a privilege usually reserved for jockeys.

'There was a world of difference in this new job,' she says, 'and I found myself riding and schooling alongside some of the magical names of racing, some of the top jockeys of the day.'

She married Richard Pitman a year later, in October 1965, and they went to live in a small cottage owned by the trainer Fulke Walwyn. When son Mark appeared 10 months later they bought a bungalow. It was a tight enough squeeze for three, but after Paul was born, it became well nigh intolerable. Being a young mother with two small children cooped up all day in a tiny bungalow was depressing for a free, energetic spirit. Worst of all, there were no horses in her life.

The bleakness of this period is eloquently conveyed in her autobiography. 'I was a wild New Forest pony shut up in a stable. I was a free child trapped and ensnared. I endured terrible depression, and though the doctor might have felt that a handful of tranquillizers would relieve me of these feelings, I knew they could not. It was unlikely I would be able to endure such a life for very long.'

Thankfully, Richard's career as a jockey began to blossom at about this time and they were able to buy, with the help of a loan from Lord Cadogan (whose horses Richard rode), their own small livery stables at Hinton Parva. The business of livery stables at that time was to house and care for hunters and hacks. The idea behind the Parva Stud, as Jenny christened it, was to specialize at the very top end of the livery market by offering to take in racehorses that were either injured or broken down and nurse them back to health.

It was a great idea. No one had tried that before and Jenny, with her experience in helping her father look after ponies in Hoby, was ideally suited to the task. It was her business because Richard was still working more or less full time for Fred Winter. It was Winter who became the first customer and others soon followed, including some 'rogue' horses that had lost their appetite for racing. Within a year Jenny began training point-to-pointers and notched up her first win as a trainer at Tweseldown point-to-point, near Aldershot. In her first season she fielded 14 runners, of which nine won and two came second.

For a while the careers of both Pitmans flourished, but by the time Jenny gained her Jockey Club licence as a National Hunt trainer, Richard had quit racing to become a BBC TV commentator and the marriage was showing signs of strain. In the summer of 1976 they separated, Parva Stud was sold for £40,000, and with her share Jenny bought the tumbledown Weathercock House in Upper Lambourn, which has been the home of Jenny Pitman Racing Ltd ever since.

## Entrepreneur!

After a brief reunion in 1977, Jenny and Richard parted for good. She took it very hard, and though she is not the kind to waste too much energy on bitterness, she still harbours anger. A messy and expensive divorce settlement added considerably to the financial implications of the debacle.

'I was just starting,' she remembers. 'At one stage I thought of packing it up and getting a job in a shoe shop, so I'd have a guaranteed income. I felt I shouldn't put my desire to work with horses above the security of the kids. The problem, even today, is that you never know from one month to the next what your income's going to be. My income rises and falls by the success of my horses.

'Fred Winter persuaded me. One day, when I was talking about giving up, he gave me the most serious bollocking I've ever had — if it hadn't been for Fred, I probably would not have carried on.' Though she had her licence by then and had won her first major race — the Midlands National with Watafella — she was very aware of how hard it was going to be to make a living for three.

'There are very few women trainers; I always felt you had to achieve four times as much to get half the recognition for the winners you trained.'

She attributes her decision to embark on a full-time career as a National Hunt trainer to a classic mixture of necessity and chance. The necessity was clear enough. 'I needed to be responsible for and to bring up two kids. They were at prep school at the time of the split. I wanted things to stay as normal as possible.'

The chance came in the form of a request from Tony Stratton-Smith, managing director of Charisma Records, to look after his horse, Biretta, who had joint problems. Jenny was very flattered — 'Tony had more belief in me than I had in myself' — and set about Biretta's restoration. She qualified him for point-to-pointing, but thought he was good enough to win a hunter 'chase (halfway between point-to-pointing and full National Hunt). She was right. He finished second in his first race but Jenny, in an early display of toughness and professionalism, lodged an objection to the winner for 'taking our ground', and Biretta was declared the winner.

'I didn't want to run a business,' she says. 'I enjoyed going to the races, watching and then going back. But I needed to stay alive. Tony wanted me to work for him. I was flattered he had that confidence in me, but I didn't like the idea of being wholly dependent on him. So, all of a sudden, I was in this pond and I had to stop from drowning.

'The nice thing was that I didn't have a lot of horses when the boys were at school so I had time to go and watch them play rugby, cricket and football. At that time the yard was smaller. That may have been the best period of all — I had time off in the afternoon. Now, if I leave, there's so much to do that it can become a headache.'

As a role model for **Andreas Whittam Smith**, Eddie Shah was flawed because he wasn't a journalist.

'I admire Eddie Shah enormously. He saw a flower where there was only desert. But I thought, "Why should it be these ruddy tycoons? Why not journalists?" I was affronted.'

In March 1985, two days after Eddie Shah announced his plan to launch a new national tabloid newspaper, *Today*, using new technology, Whittam Smith was rung up by a *Business Week* journalist seeking the views of the *Daily Telegraph*'s distinguished City editor on the chances for Shah's project.

'I told him it couldn't succeed,' Whittam Smith recalls, 'and then I thought about it and decided I was wrong.'

He was in one of his 'annoyed' moods at the time. The *Daily Telegraph*'s circulation was falling, and the increasingly desperate attempts of its owner, Lord Hartwell, to raise money had sapped morale and created a mood of uncertainty. Whittam Smith liked Hartwell, but he found it annoying to be working for an owner who seemed to have little understanding of the economics of modern newspapers, and who appeared ready to surrender control of the company to the Canadian entrepreneur Conrad Black for a knock-down price.

But Whittam Smith is an ambitious man and he thought he had some chance of succeeding Bill Deedes, then 71, as editor of the *Daily Telegraph*. He wanted the job badly, so he felt it would be unwise to be too outspoken about his feelings.

'I was worried about the *Daily Telegraph*, so I got hold of a prospectus [for Hartwell's fund-raising]. I did some sums and worked out that if 1 per cent of the *Daily Telegraph*'s readers took up the minimum of £500 for a Business Expansion Scheme investment, you'd have £6 million. If you weren't careful, it might have been £30 million.'

Whittam Smith thinks such back-of-the-envelope calculations are a fine test of a business idea. 'If you can't put it on the back of an envelope,' he insists, 'it probably won't work.'

On 14 May, two months after Shah's announcement and with the idea that was to become the *Independent* already well rooted in his mind, Whittam Smith wrote to Hartwell proposing the BES plan and suggesting an executive share option scheme and a restructuring of the board to reflect the new ownership pattern. The ideas were rejected.

Whittam Smith was annoyed. He says now that if Hartwell had agreed to the BES offer, he would probably not have left to set up a rival paper. Meanwhile, his interest in Shah's project was growing. 'I've always had a twin-track mind,' he says. 'I like to advance in two roughly parallel directions at the same time.' He also prides himself on his ability to spot turning points in business and politics.

Whittam Smith had not thought about new newspapers before the Shah announcement, but he does admit to a feeling of growing anger about the way Fleet Street was being hijacked by what he saw as a bunch of bandits. 'I felt that very strongly. I was fed up with them.'

The more he thought about the idea of an editorially-led new newspaper project, the more convinced he became that destiny was calling him, and only him. 'I felt all the lines converged on me. It was only possible at a time of fundamental change in the industry – a once-in-a-lifetime upheaval, like the new technology. The only person capable of raising money, and who also knew enough about newspapers, would be a financial journalist. I found it hard to imagine how any other kind of journalist could do it. It would be like sending a non-Chinese speaker to be a spy in Peking.'

So it had to be done immediately, while the advent of new technology offered a window of opportunity and it could only be done by a financial journalist. The third indicator that Whittam Smith felt to be pointing at him was his conviction that this financial journalist would have to be 'reasonably well established'.

With this sense of destiny, Whittam Smith set about the task of turning the idea into a plan. He had breakfast with Shah on 22 March and rang Graeme Walsh at Morgan Grenfell, the City merchant bank (and a member of the Accepting Houses Committee), to ask if he thought a £10 million newspaper project could be financed. Walsh said, 'Yes, subject to 1,000 conditions.'

While editing the *Telegraph*'s City pages, Whittam Smith wrote memos to himself which record how the bones of his idea became flesh. By the end of March he had decided the newspaper would be a national broadsheet, would appeal to younger readers, be 'strongly libertarian', have an edition at midnight, the average age of staff would be about 35 (no one over 50), there would be no distinction between sub-editors and writers, employees would all have shares, journalists would have control, and all the new technology, including full-page, on-screen layout, would be used.

He felt the editorial stance should reflect a belief in free-market economics and there should be an emphasis on news. He also pencilled in weekly coverage of science, technology and education and on 31 March he wrote: 'I am now inclined to think that proclaiming an independent standpoint is actually marking a definite position on the political spectrum.'

He was acutely aware of how dependent quality national newspapers are on advertising, so he went to the top, as usual, and approached Maurice Saatchi, who arranged a meeting between Whittam Smith and Saatchi's chief media buyer, John

Perris. This was a key test, for it would be men like Perris who would hold the fate of the project in their hands. Whittam Smith convinced him and Saatchis agreed to help with market research on a 'no foal, no fee' basis.

By now it was time for team-building. He thought highly of Matthew Symonds, the *Telegraph*'s economic leader writer, and had lunch with him on 1 April. Symonds agreed to join, and Douglas Long, who had retired as chief executive of Mirror Group Newspapers the previous year, signed up later that month. In June, Stephen Glover, a feature and leader writer at the *Telegraph* became the fourth member of the team.

It is interesting that throughout this period the project remained secret and, in view of Whittam Smith's insistence that he would probably have abandoned the plan had Hartwell responded positively to his mid-May memo about rescuing the *Telegraph*, it also remained provisional. There might have been disappointment if the project had aborted then, but no boats would have been burned.

As it was, the project had gathered considerable momentum by the time the *Sunday Times* revealed the existence of a secret, £30 million new newspaper project on 22 December and the *Financial Times* named names on Friday, 27 December. They had committed themselves to 'go for it' in September, and when Whittam Smith, Symonds and Glover finally resigned from the *Daily Telegraph* on 28 December, fund-raising for the initial £2 million planning phase was well advanced.

Later, Whittam Smith likened the exercise, from Eddie Shah's seminal announcement in March 1985, to the completion of the second (£16 million) financing round on 17 April 1986 to crossing 1,000 bridges.

'It must have been terribly exciting,' I suggested. Whittam Smith smiled. 'If you could ask a climber when he's inching up a rock face whether it's exciting, he'd say, "Yes, but that's not my emotion at this moment — I'm cold, exhausted and I just want to get on to this next ledge. But, yes, I volunteered." You shouldn't start anything unless you can bear the failure.'

Typically, Whittam Smith was deliberate and systematic

about confronting his own personal downside. 'I calculated that if I failed, I would lose my job as City editor and probably my house, too, because I'd taken out a second mortgage, but that I would regain employment. I had no qualms about going to someone like Hamish [Macrae, then City editor of the *Guardian* and now associate editor of the *Independent*] and asking for a job. I thought I would get it, too. I knew I could have put up with it. My wife and family were very supportive throughout.'

The term 'larger than life' fits **Bob Payton** like a glove, and entrepreneurs like him can make it without strong role models.

With the benefit of hindsight, one could argue that Payton's entrepreneurial awakening was the product of two passions – for Chicago and pizza; two problems – he was an expatriate and he lacked the sycophancy to succeed as an account director in advertising; and two predispositions – to see opportunities, where others only saw problems, and to entertain.

He was also blessed with a sensitive cultural antenna, which was soon put to good use at JWT's London office. Payton developed a special act for the agency's more conservative clients to persuade them of the importance of the new youth culture. He would dress up in his ad-agency suit, go into a dance routine on the office carpet, and then urge the bemused clients that it was time to 'get down and boogie'.

Despite this fundamentally irreverent attitude to clients, Payton's strengths were recognized by JWT. He was appointed an associate director, and worked as account director on key accounts, such as Gillette, Kraft, Beecham and Berger Paints (now part of Williams Holdings).

In 1977 he was offered a job in JWT's New York office at a princely salary of $75,000 a year. As he remarked to Kippenburger and Burns, 'They'd recognized an entrepreneurial streak in me and wanted me to head up a new division. They felt that I wasn't any good at saying "Yes sir, no sir" to clients. I've never been good at bowing and scraping to people, and advertising has a lot of that in it. Instead they wanted me to go and build up this division. The trouble was it meant calling on chairmen and presidents of companies back in the States. That didn't appeal either.' If it had been Chicago rather than New York, that might have been different.

By then, London had hooked him. He hadn't liked it at first, but he realized after a while that although there was less money around, there was something about the quality of life in England that appealed to him. He had written *The Chicagoan's Tour Guide to London*, had a comfortable flat near Oxford Circus, and was in the habit of riding his bicycle out to Brick Lane and Covent Garden markets on Sunday mornings. 'One morning, I woke up and knew I had quality of life. I really got into it. I liked the easy and relaxed atmosphere, and the fact that nobody ever stole my bike. I didn't want to go to New York.'

Payton had always been fond of dining out, but he was no fan of London restaurants. 'I used to talk to friends when they came over from America about how wonderful the Due pizzas were in Chicago. They had been serving these deep-dish pizzas there since 1945. At the Pizza Express in Fulham we needed 13 pizzas between four of us.'

He attributes his success to his creation, with the help of other restaurants like Hard Rock and Joe Allen's, of what he calls 'a street-food culture' in Britain. 'You go to any city in the US and people will tell you that if you want a good meal, go to Ed's. There was nothing like that here. Fish and chips, and soggy cornish pasties don't add up to a street-food culture.'

But things were changing in 1977. Kentucky Fried Chicken had been franchised in 1965, Peter Boizot's Pizza Express chain was flourishing, the Great American Disaster in Fulham (not to be confused with the much less successful Great American Success in Kensington) opened in 1969, Isaac Tygrett's Hard Rock Café hit Hyde Park Corner two years later and the first McDonald's had opened its doors in Woolwich in 1974.

The big gap, as Payton saw it, was deep-dish pizza served in a Chicagoan atmosphere, 'whose pizzas would be to Pizzaland what the Hard Rock Café hamburger was to Wimpy'.

The idea began to crystallize into a plan when he was introduced by his accountant in Chicago to Laurie Soll, who had recently opened a Chicago Pizza restaurant in Los Angeles. He offered Soll $5,000 to teach him the craft of Chicago pizza-making, and began looking for a site and the necessary finance for a London restaurant. It was not easy.

'I knew what I liked and was willing to bet the ranch that what I liked, everyone would like. But no one would back me. EMI was going to do it for a while, but then they turned it down.' The EMI rejection letter, received on 1 July, the day Payton left JWT, was later framed and hangs in the foyer of My Kinda Holdings' head office in London.

But Payton was committed by then. The pizza ovens had been ordered, his mentor Laurie Soll and his wife were on their way to help with the launch, the break with JWT was a *fait accompli* and he wasn't about to go cap in hand to ask for his job back. His entrepreneurial spirit was awakened now and the only begging he would do was with bankers and venture capitalists.

Few entrepreneurs, when looking back over their careers, do not fulminate against one venture capital fund or another. They regard each rejection as a personal affront and are so convinced by the strength of their own business ideas that they are astonished when others fail to see how brilliant they are. But they like the venture capitalists who back them. Payton says the late Tony Lorenz, whose ECI Ventures was to back his projects, 'was a great friend'.

Eventually, in 1977, Payton won backing from Norton Warburg. 'I had gone out with Andrew Warburg's secretary for a while,' Payton recalls, 'and they were just setting up their venture capital division.' When Norton Warburg went belly up in 1979, the Chicago Pizza Pie Factory was one of only two good investments held by its venture fund. With APA's backing, Bob Payton bought the shares from the receivers and emerged with 75 per cent of the equity.

He had always wanted majority control, having been in a minority under the original Norton Warburg arrangement, with an option to buy a majority later. 'I don't like not being in control,' he says. 'I don't mind having a minority as long as I'm running the show.'

# Reflections

Each of these stories of entrepreneurial awakening involved role models. Richard Noble's idols were the two Campbells and John Cobb; Clive Sinclair was midwife to Chris Curry's entrepreneurial career; Martin Sorrell's stints with Ralph Glendinning, Mark McCormack, James Gulliver and the Saatchi brothers gave a background plausibility to his own enterprising adventures; Brian McGowan was influenced by men like Jim Slater and Jock Mackenzie; Keith Duckworth's entrepreneurial model was Colin Chapman; Jenny Pitman was goaded by men like Chris Taylor and Fred Winter; Andreas Whittam Smith acknowledges a great debt to Eddie Shah; Bob Payton's mentor was Laurie Soll and his models were the Hard Rock Café in London and Due's in Chicago.

But apart, perhaps, from Richard Noble's idols, none of these role models were heroes. Their weaknesses, in most cases, were more powerful stimuli for their followers than their strengths. And none of these key providers of background plausibility could ever have been sufficient on their own to induce our eight entrepreneurs to step across the threshold into the entrepreneurial life.

Other factors also contributed to the decision to take that crucial step, including luck, timing and the circumstances of their lives that made the value of an improbable dream more attractive to them than the probable extrapolation of an unsatisfactory present.

Whittam Smith's metaphor of 1,000 bridges, each of which had to be crossed on the road to the realization of his dream, is a striking one. Other entrepreneurs have likened their experiences to driving down a street with frequent traffic lights, all of which had to be green at the appropriate time if their progress was to be maintained.

The stories of those thousands of aspiring entrepreneurs who failed to negotiate a bridge, or who encountered a red light and had to stop, are seldom told. Only the stories of those who made it can emerge from the ferment of entrepreneurial endeavour to become examples of what can be achieved with a mixture of determination, daring, diligence and luck.

Crossing the threshold into the entrepreneurial life and starting the journey that begins on the other side opens up a new set of opportunities. Those who make it are often those who take each step at a time and who have a flexible itinerary.

The story of Richard Branson's career is one example. His initial enterprise, *Student*, failed, but it acted as a launch-pad for his second career in retailing. This in turn led to the recording studio, the record business, to videos, films, television and, less directly, to an airline.

Anita Roddick also pursued a remarkably circuitous route to her huge success as a specialist retailer. She and husband Gordon began with a hotel, progressed to an Italian healthfood restaurant, which was transformed, when it bombed, into a successful hamburger joint and then, when that proved too exhausting and Gordon decided to ride his horse from Buenos Aires to New York, Anita decided to open 'a little shop'.

In her autobiography Roddick says that what saved them so frequently 'was our willingness to recognize that we were wrong and our ability to move swiftly on to the next idea'.

But there is also a requirement to keep looking forward. One important feature of the entrepreneurial threshold is that, once crossed, it follows the traveller. At every junction in the road, and at every obstacle, there is the option to step backwards. Whittam Smith was very conscious of it and was ready to take it if the *Independent* project had foundered.

Others never look back. It is the status of the entrepreneur they are committed to, not a particular project. Payton knew, once set on his course, that he could never go back to being a subordinate. Duckworth's determination to keep his company

**Entrepreneur!**

alive indicated that he, too, never gave much thought to the idea of admitting defeat and of stepping back over the threshold.

Being an entrepreneur, and tasting even a little of what it means, changes you. You become trapped in the flood-tide of your affairs, whether or not it leads on to fortune. Some say it makes you unemployable afterwards, and that former entrepreneurs are either dead or out of work.

# CHAPTER 3
# The business

# CHAPTER 3

# The business

People who create and build up businesses tend to acquire a far deeper understanding of what business is and how firms interact with and extract nourishment from the economic, social and political environments in which they live, than those who spend all their working lives as the employees of large firms.

Even when the entrepreneur's company fails, there are always important lessons to be learned. Some say you learn far more from your failures than from your successes. I know from my own experience that a personal encounter with the intrinsic mortality of companies can leave a deep impression.

Entrepreneurs are therefore well placed to learn some of the secrets of business success. Their perceptions of what matters are not obscured by the impression of solidity and durability that a few large, well-established organizations give to the majority of people who work for them. They know that it is in the nature of companies to struggle, and sometimes to fail.

The purpose of this chapter is to try to glean some insight from our eight entrepreneurs into what mattered to them in their careers as company builders — what it was that enabled them to succeed, or caused them to fail.

The story of how the *Independent* — conceived, realized and managed by a bunch of the 'journos' that tycoons like Rupert Murdoch regarded with such scorn — took on those tycoons and won is well known. It's *Boy's Own* stuff for journalists, even for those of us who had nothing to do with the *Independent*. It gave us a self-respect and sense of ownership of our industry that we had lost when the new breed of tycoons had moved in and started pushing us around.

**Andreas Whittam Smith,** by showing that if journalists are pushed too far by predatory or incompetent proprietors they can become formidable competitors, changed the balance of power in the whole newspaper industry.

The first issue of the *Independent* appeared on Tuesday, 7 October 1986. Over 650,000 copies were printed and all were sold. First issues almost always sell well because of their curiosity value, but no one believed that circulation would be maintained. The initial target was a stable 375,000 at which Newspaper Publishing plc was expected to break even.

In his launch statement Whittam Smith explained the strategy that had informed his bold adventure. 'The *Independent* exists because of a shared belief on the part of its investors and the people who work for it that the readers of quality newspapers are not well served and that journalism of the highest standard cannot easily flourish when impeded by union restrictive practices or by the political prejudices of the typical newspaper proprietor.'

Editors of rival quality dailies were predictably scathing. Max Hastings of the *Daily Telegraph* judged the paper 'respectable, honourable, responsible, pretty dull', and predicted that 'when it has its financial crisis, some rich sugar daddy will come along and rescue it'.

Peter Preston, of the *Guardian*, which would soon be goaded by the newcomer's success into a major redesign, said it reminded him of *The Times* of five years ago: 'They need to offer something absolutely different. This is absolutely the same.'

Charles Wilson, of *The Times*, said: 'The paper lacks the

natural spirit, character and personality of an established paper.'

Big advertisers, a less partisan and much more important audience, were more sanguine. Bill Jones, press-buying director at Davidson Pearce, said: 'As an initial offering, it's outstanding. It has a spark to it that the other qualities don't have.'

Robert Dodds, media director at BBDO (UK), predicted the new paper would do brilliantly: 'The layout is fabulous and it's a good, easy read.'

Brian Jacobs, media director at Leo Burnett, also enthused: 'The biggest compliment I can pay is that it didn't look like a first issue.'

The Jacobs judgement, a mirror image of Charles Wilson's, was particularly perceptive. The great achievement of the *Independent* was the speed with which it established itself as an institution. In an analysis of the national newspaper industry in May 1990 I showed that the newest UK quality daily had by then achieved the strongest 'brand' of all.

In a year in which total quality daily circulation fell 1.3 per cent, the circulation of the *Independent* rose 2.2 per cent, despite the fact that it had spent, on average, only 67p per unit of circulation on promotion during the previous two years. This compared with 235p for *The Times*, 272p for the *Daily Telegraph* and 297p for the *Guardian*. The *Financial Times* achieved a 0.1 per cent circulation rise, with an average annual promotional spend of 179p per customer.

As Max Hastings predicted, Newspaper Publishing has had its financial crisis but has yet to be bought by a sugar daddy, unless La Repubblica International (owner of *La Repubblica* newspaper in Italy) and Promotora de Informaciones (owner of *El Pais* in Spain) can be counted as such.

Following a £22 million refinancing in the summer of 1990, the Italian and Spanish groups emerged as the largest shareholders, with 14.9 per cent apiece of Newspaper Publishing – just under the original 15 per cent limit for individual holdings Whittam Smith had insisted on.

The need for a further £16 million refinancing in September

1991 required the limit on individual shareholdings to be raised, but even after this the Italian and Spanish companies spoke for only 18.04 per cent of the equity each.

The advertising recession, beginning in early 1990 and still showing little signs of bottoming out at the time of writing, was one half of the reason for the company's heavy losses in 1990 and 1991. The other half was the launch of the *Independent on Sunday* in February 1990. In terms of circulation, it must rank as a success, if not quite on a par with that of the main paper, but financially it has been crippling.

Critics say the timing, partly prompted by the launch of the now failed *Sunday Correspondent*, was disastrous and that Whittam Smith should have admitted his mistake and closed it. Even some within the company still see his insistence on persevering with the 'Sindie', as the Sunday edition is known, as more foolhardy than courageous.

There is a theory, proposed at length in the *Evening Standard Magazine* in late 1991, that the survival of the *Independent* itself was placed in jeopardy by Whittam Smith's handling of the Sindie affair. Stephen Glover, one of Newspaper Publishing's founders, had been appointed editor of the new paper. When it struggled to reach break-even in difficult market conditions, he proposed a partial buy-out of the Sindie. Whittam Smith rejected the idea, Glover resigned, the Sindie operations were merged with those of the *Independent* and an alternative, 'might-have-been-if-only-Andreas-hadn't-been-so-stubborn' history of Newspaper Publishing had been written.

All institutions it seems, even new ones, acquire with their brand value an internal political system. It is as if the sheer strength of the brand liberates the company from its dependence on founders, and extends a licence to others to claim ownership of the achievement. 'Just because he started it doesn't mean he always knows what's best for it,' is the claim.

But if the *Independent on Sunday* survives and climbs out of the recession alongside its rivals, Newspaper Publishing will have a strong contender in the most profitable segment of the quality market, and folly will become courage again.

Whittam Smith conveyed his mood to the *Financial Times* at the time of the refinancing. 'We're like a destroyer escorting an Atlantic convoy in the war. We're battered, shot up and the paint is peeling, but we're close to port and all the guns are still working.'

He is philosophical about the way fate has dealt with him in the first five years of his entrepreneurial career. 'I have nothing to complain about. I've had some aces and I've had some twos.'

What do you do after you've realized your childhood dream? It would have been possible for **Richard Noble** to try to break his own land speed record, but it would have been difficult.

'Donald Campbell ran a record-breaking industry. He'd always left a little bit of room so he could beat it next time. We'd gone as fast as we could with that technology. There was nothing left. British Airways offered us a Concorde engine, but its power to weight ratio wasn't much better than the Avon's, so we would have ended up with a larger car and the same performance. And you can't switch a team like that into making things. It had to be disbanded. We sold everything and divided the proceeds between us. The car's in a museum.'

Part of Noble's training for the LSR attempt was learning to fly. 'I got hooked,' he says, 'but I couldn't see why flying was so expensive. The answer was the cost of maintaining very old aeroplanes. If the 25,000 planes used by the flying training industry around the world could be replaced by a new, lightweight plane, the cost of flying would come down. I felt there was a business opportunity for a better handling, more economical plane.'

He had a little money, so he established a new and unproven team on the Isle of Wight and got the project started. Then he began looking for finance.

'I went round all the normal institutional sources. There was a barrage of "no's". People didn't understand and they didn't seem to want to understand. The aviation business was seen as high risk. The enterprise industry looks for a return of 40 per cent. That is very difficult to achieve in manufacturing, but I managed to make the business plan work. I knew there was a solid opportunity if we could crack it because a plane like that could be in production for 20 years.'

The ARV Super 2, as Noble's plane was called, was a light-weight, shoulder-wing monoplane powered by a brand new engine designed by Mike Hewland, the very successful manufac-turer of racing gearboxes.

'An aeroplane is a system, of which the expensive bit is the airframe. The size of structure is directly related to engine weight. The old-technology, off-the-shelf engines were very heavy. If we'd used one, our plane would have been the same size as the old aircraft and with similar performance. It would not be competitive with the old, fully depreciated trainers. We were the first to use superplastic aluminium in the fuselage structure and forward-swept wings, and Mike Hewland developed a liquid-cooled, geared 2-stroke engine, weighing 100 pounds and developing 75 hp.'

Noble thought of raising the money through a BES issue and a USM flotation, but feared the likely institutional response would have doomed the venture at birth. He tried to find a way to reduce the project risk progressively, until it reached a level the institutions would accept. This meant funding the project on the hoof.

'I met someone at a cocktail party and told him about it. He said, "I'm a pilot, I'll put £5,000 in." I was very concerned about the possible legal implications of this, so I discussed it in great depth with our legal advisers. Their view was that as we had been approached by a potential investor, we could send him a business plan as long as it was made clear that it was not a prospectus and that it was made plain that the project was seen as very high risk indeed.'

Noble suddenly acquired an insatiable thirst for cocktails. 'People appeared. In every case I made sure that we were approached first and each case was discussed with our legal advisers. The project qualified for BES, which was a key incen-tive. But the important thing was to be totally honest with potential investors and never to approach them. Without the private investors, the project could never have reached flying status and so never have attracted production finance.'

A prototype was completed in 13 months. British Alcan, the supplier of the superplastic aluminium for the airframe, sponsored a second plane, and the *Daily Express*, which has been a good friend of Noble's, sponsored another.

The test pilot said the plane handled beautifully, though he was nearly asphyxiated by a leaky exhaust. That was easily fixed and the project began to gather momentum. The prototype attracted more financial backing and once that was in place, Noble approached the Civil Aviation Authority for a certificate of airworthiness.

'It was a real nightmare. Until we could certificate the aeroplane we could only sell a few in kit form, so there was little revenue. The French had a competitive, government-funded aircraft which was already selling well, so we had to move quickly. The CAA charged £40 per man hour and had a surveyor for every aspect of the aircraft and its design. Nick Sibley, our chief engineer, rang me one day in complete frustration. He had a vast compliance checklist and every aspect had to be approved by the CAA before certification. The problem was the surveyors were visiting and charging, but were not making decisions.

'I can understand why the CAA is reluctant to certificate new aircraft from a new manufacturer. Aircraft losses can mean death, injury and damage; in the US this is a major legal industry. I think they assumed that like so many previous light aircraft projects, we would run out of money before the CAA had to put its name to the certificate.

'In desperation I rang the CAA chairman in midsummer and he kindly agreed to see me in November. We told the surveyors of the appointment and, suddenly, approvals started flowing. We brought the bankers to the November meeting. They very politely asked the chairman if he was ever going to certificate the aircraft. He said there were still a few problems, but, in principle, yes. The bankers left. That was all they wanted to know.

'From the moment the CAA decided we were worth support-
ing, a good relationship began to develop which eventually
resulted in certification of a very innovative aircraft in the short
period of 18 months.'

But looking back, Noble thinks the problems began before
the ultimately successful battle with the CAA bureaucrats.

'In most projects, eventual success depends crucially on the
early decisions. For instance, with ARV we did extensive and
very expensive market research which seemed to show the
market was very interested. But when we started marketing our
interpretation, there was a deep reluctance to abandon the old
ways. Perhaps they knew our window of opportunity was
limited and that if they didn't buy or lease an ARV, we would
soon be in liquidation. Even so, there were clubs who bought
Super 2s in sets of two and three aircraft.

'The project was also dependent on the engine. The aeroplane needed to be light, so we'd dedicated the airframe to the
engine. Certification was eventually achieved, but although I
was very happy with the engine, there was still considerable
prejudice against 2-strokes in aviation at the time.'

Even so, the plane started to sell and, despite a continuing
lack of money, Noble decided to gear up for production. Jigs
and tools were bought and the workforce was expanded to over
100.

'At the beginning of a project like this, you need dedicated
enthusiasts — people who are very keen and determined. The
problem is how to build that into a production team. You're
asking enthusiasts to be hard-bitten, marketing orientated managers. How do you do that and keep the entrepreneurial spirit
alive? It was fine as a little team. It started to get flaky when we
went into production.'

Noble began to feel overwhelmed. He was the entrepreneur
and because the company was under-capitalized, he had to
spend a lot of time dealing with the investors. He also had to
put the sales team together and he felt unable to delegate the
overall management role.

Then they had their first engine problems. The bearings went in some planes and they all had to be grounded. That meant refinancing and restructuring.

'We also had to bolster the management team,' Noble recalls. 'It was hard to find experienced manufacturing and manage- ment people on the Isle of Wight, and because the company wasn't profitable, people wouldn't move there.'

The second dose of engine problems — they began to fail in new planes — was terminal. The board decided to ground the plane, the organization began to fall apart, and when the investors insisted the finance director should be appointed the managing director, Noble resigned.

He admits to having made many mistakes, but he thinks they were mostly unavoidable. 'There was no way we could follow existing practice in financing and establishing the venture — it just would never have happened. It was a constant battle to persuade people to change their ways, and apart from our institutional investors, who kept the venture funded, and the project team, there seemed to be considerable external resist- ance. It was almost as if we were doing something that was indecent or illegal.

'Although the project failed, I'm very proud of what we achieved. It was a great team. I understand the ARV Super 2 is now to be built in Scotland, so if we were before our time, then we can now have the satisfaction of seeing it reborn, perhaps into a more understanding marketplace.'

It seems to me that the success of Cosworth Engineering in its first incarnation under **Keith Duckworth** rests on five pillars. The first, and most important, was Duckworth's brilliance.

If a company has resources of the kind Cosworth had 'between Duckworth's ears', as he would put it, it has a chance to do something special, like producing a racing engine so advanced when it first appeared at the Dutch Grand Prix in 1967 that it was still winning 16 years later.

Altogether, the Duckworth-designed DFV engine won 155 Grands Prix — 65 per cent of all the GPs run between 1967 and 1983. It was an astonishing achievement, unlikely ever to be repeated. It established Cosworth's reputation in the Formula 1 world and the huge success of a DFV-derivative in the Indian- apolis 500 series added, if anything, even more lustre to the Cosworth name in the US.

But brilliance, though necessary, is not sufficient for success. History is littered with the corpses of companies with brilliance – they are like shooting stars that burn brightly for a while and are then extinguished.

The second pillar of Cosworth's success, which helps explain why it survived and prospered while similar companies failed or had to be rescued, was the peculiar nature of Duckworth's aspirations. As we have seen, he started Cosworth because he thought that there was probably an interesting living to be made out of messing around with engines and racing-cars. He had no grand vision for the company and says he was as surprised as anyone else by the phenomenal success of the DFV.

'I wanted to create a company that would survive. It didn't have to be hugely profitable, but there always had to be enough money to carry on – to stay in the game we were in. I deliberately didn't expand because I thought we lacked the management skills.' However, expansion occurred because customers demanded it.

'We'd sell parts for engines that we weren't building, but we wouldn't maintain technical development. We dropped engines. But because our engines always went at least as well as we said – we were honest to a fault – we got a good name, and I was leant on to enter the market for less adequate bits.

'Cosworth Components was set up as a separate company and I tried to keep it separate, but no one believed it wasn't the same company and the costings got blurred. Even if you're in charge, you can't make it work unless people go along. They have to believe.'

Duckworth was also 'pushed' into Indianapolis 500 racing – the closest American equivalent of Formula 1 – because, although he had no wish to expand, he relished the idea of contraction even less. 'We thought F1 was going to decline, so we decided to try to get into Indy. The US racing establishment nearly forced out the DFV, but we made it. It was a forced expansion because F1 didn't decline and we had to make engines for both.'

In 1980, when Duckworth and Alf Vickers were confronting the prospect of another decline in the racing-engine market, the idea of getting into road-engines in a serious way came up. 'We reckoned that in the road-engine market you didn't need to be the brightest – just better than the rest. All the road-car makers tell tales, but in racing you can't tell tales.

'We designed a four-valve head for the Ford Pinto production engine to sell in our own right as a kit. We already had the Mercedes-Benz contract by then. Major manufacturers can't make 5,000 special engines a year – it's too small for them. Mercedes decided to make it themselves, but then it came back and we also got the work for Ford and Opel.'

It was with such reluctance that Cosworth became a designer and manufacturer of road-engines, such as the Mercedes-Benz 16V 2.3-litre, the Opel/Vauxhall 16V engine and, of course, the hugely successful 16V, turbo-charged Ford Sierra Cosworth engine, with its electrifying 220 bhp; this began life as that 'go-faster' kit for the Pinto engine.

Duckworth recalls that the Cosworth offshoot, Cosworth Castings, which makes cylinder heads for Mercedes-Benz, among many others, was also the product of a reluctant expansion. 'In 1978 we had a bad batch of castings for Indy engines – the cylinder heads melted. Casting technology was a black art at that time but manufacturers did make good batches sometimes. We thought that if we controlled all the processes carefully and kept good records, we should be able to make good batches all the time.

'We decided it was to do with the accuracy of the patterns, and with the way the moulds were filled. I liked the French Novatome magnetic pump for liquid metal in nuclear reactors – it works according to Fleming's right-hand rule. I thought it should be able to fill moulds at a programmable rate.

'Dr John Campbell introduced us to zircon sand. Silica sand has a kink in its expansion curve. Zircon's expansion curve is much smoother, so we could get more accurate castings. We patented the process.

'It wasn't part of the move into road-engines. Foundry cost effectiveness is very difficult. The technology was saleable and we wanted to expand, but it was difficult because customers want to double source.'

Duckworth's reluctance to expand also halted a possible move into bearings, but he did invest in an automatic transmission with torque converter, albeit briefly. 'I thought it might make a racing gearbox, but we stopped it when I thought it was getting to be a triumph of development over design.'

Another project axed before completion was Cosworth's own Formula 1 racing car. 'We decided that we had a good enough name for it to be safe to build a car and compete with customers. Four-wheel drive was a good opportunity, but it never worked, so we stopped the project.

'We saved a lot of money by not doing things and not going on developing things that had no chance of success. We never went into new materials like titanium con rods just because they became fashionable. Our analysis showed the advantages to be negligible and manufacture was difficult, as well as expensive. I stopped several developments because it looked as if they were going to take too long and cost too much. In quite a few of these cases I was probably wrong and we should have carried on.

'Colin Chapman gave me a good metaphor for a company. It is a colander in which the holes are costs and inefficiencies. There's a tap at the top pouring water in — that's revenue. Profit is what flows over the rim. You can turn on the tap or plug the holes. I'm a hole-plugger. The market might look okay now, but what happens later? My markets are very variable and plus or minus 10 per cent can have a plus or minus 50 per cent impact on profit.'

The third pillar of Cosworth's success was Keith Duckworth's almost puritanical attitude to debt. He thinks borrowing is immoral, and since he was never driven by a lust for profit, he was never forced into losses or into debt.

Cosworth made a £744 loss in its first year to 30 September

1959 because Duckworth bought a dynamometer, but it's been profitable ever since. In 1967, the year Jim Clark drove the new DFV-powered Lotus 49 to victory in the Dutch Grand Prix, it employed 50 people and made £36,145 pre-tax on sales of £347,407. In the year to 31 January 1990 Cosworth recorded pre-tax profits of £14 million on sales of £53 million, and employed 750 people.

The fourth pillar of Cosworth's success is its relationship with Ford. It began in the late 1950s when Duckworth rewrote the textbooks on camshaft design with his modifications of the Ford 105E engine for Formula Junior racing. This led to contract work on other Ford engines, including the Cortina GT engine, and the twin-cam engine in the Lotus Cortina.

Ford's faith in Duckworth's ability to extract extra power from its engines led to its decision in 1966 to ask Cosworth to design and develop a new F1 engine. That became the DFV. The contract price of £100,000 must rank as the best racing-engine investment ever made.

After the huge success of the Sierra Cosworth and the recent launch of the Cosworth-powered Scorpio, the company has moved even closer to the Ford mainstream. There is talk of Cosworth engines for variants of Ford's US cars once the new Cosworth XBA engine has reclaimed, with the help of American actor Paul Newman's Newman-Haas team, the dominance of Indy racing the DFV had achieved in the 1970s.

Why did this close business relationship, which now accounts for 70 per cent of Cosworth's turnover, never become a marriage? The answer is simple. Duckworth didn't want to sell, and when Cosworth came up for auction in 1990, after the acquisition of UEI by Carlton Communications, Ford didn't want to buy.

'We thought about it,' says Ford's motor sport chief, Mike Kranefuss, 'but we felt we'd be too stifling — that we'd hand-cuff it. Cosworth lives and thrives on its unique position in the sector. Its reputation and its image of being successful enhance our products. We need Cosworth, and they need us.'

The fifth pillar of Cosworth's success was the way in which

Duckworth managed his know-how capital. 'I always under-employed a lot of people because doing things to a much higher standard needed better people. It requires 20 per cent of the people to do 80 per cent of the job well, and 80 per cent of the people to do the rest. It is possible, very rapidly, to change it to doing five times more reasonably well. That, I venture to suggest, is what's happening now.'

Another aspect of Duckworth's skilful management of know-how was the Cosworth habit of thinking things out.

'Pencil is very easy to rub out,' Duckworth grins. 'We needed to be fairly certain about a design before we built it. As a result, we didn't need to do much development. I like to get it right first time. That's why some others went broke. They spent too much on experiment. But maybe that was really the best way because I'm very rare and my hourly rate might be so high that trial and error would be cheaper.'

Duckworth retired as Cosworth chairman in 1988 but stayed on as a consultant for another year. 'I was fed up not being able to convince people. I tried to fight for a course of action that was essential. I failed, and I couldn't be bothered to fight any more.'

He wouldn't be drawn further on what is obviously a painful subject, but it is clear that he remains very interested in how Cosworth is faring under the wing of its third parent, Vickers.

'It looks the same, but it's totally different. It's now part of a public company and the pressure to make a profit must be high. There's a temptation to take any job that comes along. It's not wedded to perfection. That's good for some people – there are more job opportunities; they're not being held down. I think they've done it very well, but if you're a subsidiary of a public company, you cannot possibly run a company in a long-term fashion.'

The Chicago Pizza Pie Factory was opened on Thanksgiving Day, 28 November 1977, in Crown Passage, a narrow alley off Pall Mall. It was the product, not of market research, but of **Bob Payton**'s conviction that what he liked, others would like. The place reeked of Chicago. The walls were covered with Chicago memorabilia, and the multi-speaker sound system pumped out tapes of a Chicago radio station, punctuated every hour and a half by Frank Sinatra's version of 'Chicago'.

The restaurant was owned by My Kinda Holdings, Payton's holding company, and within days of its opening it was the 'hot' place. Queues for the 100 seats formed at lunchtime and in the evening, and within six weeks it had reached break-even.

The menu was simple – garlic bread or stuffed mushrooms, then deep-dish pizza in two sizes (large or huge), accompanied by American-style salads. For afters there was chocolate and banana cheesecake, and it was all washed down with Coca-Cola or American Schlitz beer.

The partnership with Laurie Soll worked well for a while but after a year, Soll left and opened L.S. Grunts Chicago Pizza Co. in Covent Garden.

Payton was very conscious of the value of his style and was very jealous of it. He sued his erstwhile friend and mentor, alleging 'passing off', but lost, after a messy court case. He remained a determined litigant, however, in protecting what he regarded as his personal intellectual property. By the end of 1980 he had settled out of court twice, and was planning to take action against two more imitators. He also took full-page advertisements in *Caterer and Hotelkeeper*, warning would-be copycats of dire legal consequences.

By 1979 the restaurant had outgrown Crown Passage and moved to its present site in Hanover Square. A year later a second Chicago Pizza Pie Factory opened in Bath, and soon Payton was plotting another cultural import from America, barbecue ribs. 'We ate in 85 restaurants in 10 cities to find the products we wanted to produce in London.'

The Chicago Rib Shack opened in Knightsbridge in February 1982. By the end of that year the three restaurants were serving 14,000 customers a week and generating an annual turnover of £4 million.

The remarkable feature of this period was that, while Payton was energetically opening and running successful businesses, he was in an almost constant state of financial crisis. In addition to the collapse of Norton Warburg, Payton had to cope with sceptical bankers, a serious fire at the Bath site and a slower than expected build-up of custom at the Rib Shack. He was constantly having to juggle with creditors and cash-flow, and the company might have folded in the summer of 1982 if the Rib Shack hadn't come good in the nick of time.

But the crisis passed, and a refinancing in August 1982, in partnership with Ronald Cohen's APA fund, left Payton with 75 per cent of a highly profitable business and a determination to grapple with what he saw as the disaster area of the English pub.

Henry J. Bean's, But His Friends All Call Him Hank, Bar and Grill (it's in *The Guinness Book of Records* as the pub with the longest name) opened in Abingdon Road, Kensington, in November 1983, and another Paytonized pub of the same name soon followed in Chelsea. Both were very successful.

After pizzas, ribs and pubs came fish. Payton Plaice, a 250-seat seafood restaurant, opened in Charing Cross Road, in November 1984. Payton admits he made mistakes with Payton Plaice. He told Burns and Kippenberger: 'In particular, I got the image wrong because I said that having taught the English how to eat American food, I'm going to teach them how to eat fish and chips properly! It was absolutely the wrong thing to say.'

After a rocky joint venture attempt with the Chicago Pizza Pie in Barcelona, Payton launched his frontal assault on Europe in early 1985, with the opening of the Chicago Pizza Pie Factory in rue de Berri, near the Champs Elysées in Paris. It was an instant success and Payton still regards it as one of his most satisfying achievements.

The Bath restaurant was sold, but problems with his Spanish partners led, indirectly, to the opening of another Henry J. Bean's in Barcelona. By early 1985 there were eight restaurants and bars in the group – five in London, two in Barcelona and one in Paris. Payton decided to take it easy.

He was living in Leicestershire in a converted school and learning to ride, when he saw Stapleford Park, a large, sixteenth-century mansion near Melton Mowbray. He bought it for £750,000 and decided to turn it into a country hotel. It was hard to find the money, but once Payton has an idea in his head, it stays there. With more help from A P A and from a number of new backers, including E C I, the hotel opened in 1988 and another feather waved jauntily in Payton's cap.

Stapleford Park was an important move because it made space in My Kinda Town for Payton's friend Peter Webber, whom he had been trying to seduce away from the Imperial Group for years. Webber had always felt Payton's holding company lacked the room for both of them, but when Hanson bought Imperial in 1986, and Courage was sold to Trusthouse Forte, Webber became more amenable. It also seemed that Payton's preoccupation with Stapleford Park would give Webber the space he needed to run the rest of the business.

In the early Stapleford Park days Payton thought that it would be a project to keep him occupied for a decade, but when I spoke to him three years later, the 35-bedroom hotel had just been put on the market. 'It will be sold as a business,' says Payton. 'It needed my drive and vision to start it, but now it works. I feel I've done that. I'm in the throes of getting pregnant again.'

One of the reasons for Payton's success as a restaurateur is his timing. My Kinda Town was conceived on the eve of the Thatcher era and developed during the 1980s. It was a time of profound change in British society. People were becoming more prosperous, but also more pressurized. Modern life was more complicated and very busy. There was a hunger for the new, but also an appetite for the simple. At the same time there was a new fascination with American culture, particularly in London. Large numbers of US banks had flocked to the City following financial deregulation, and American accents seemed to be everywhere. My Kinda Town was a reflection of this new mood, and of the acuteness with which Payton felt it.

'People want quality and simplicity,' he says. 'If you spend a day struggling to get a modem to work, you're frustrated. The angriest I've been for some time was when I was talking on the car phone recently and got cut off. People's lives are so full of complex technology they don't want to plough through elaborate meals and complicated menus. They want to be entertained and I'm in the entertainment business.'

I asked him whether he was planning to float My Kinda Town on the Stock Exchange. 'Go public? Not me, pal. I'm working too hard to have time to look after guys in the City. They want love, but they're a band of whores, prepared to turn their backs as soon as you get into hot water.' I wonder how Payton's outside investors will feel about that when they begin to seek an 'exit route'.

When **Martin Sorrell** and his partner, Preston Rabl, bought a stake in a Kent wire basket manufacturer in 1985, the smart money in the City drove WPP's shares up sharply. But even the most sanguine of Sorrell followers could not have anticipated the sheer speed with which events were to unfold. It was as if Sorrell had worked it all out long ago, and all he had to do when he moved to WPP full time in 1986 was to press the button.

He had seen the flaws in the Saatchi & Saatchi vision of a global business services group embracing everything from advertising to management consultancy, and was determined to adopt a narrower focus at WPP. Marketing services (rather than the wider business services) was his chosen hunting ground, and at first he concentrated his acquisitive efforts, using cash, shares and the earn-out system he'd pioneered at Saatchis, on so-called 'below-the-line' marketing. Some say the narrow focus was because he'd promised the Saatchis he wouldn't compete directly with them in advertising.

Be that as it may, until mid-1987 WPP satisfied its hunger for acquisitions with a handful of small design and sales promotion consultancies in the UK and the US. Sorrell feels at home in the US and finds it easier to do business there. It was always part of the plan.

I was shocked when WPP launched a hostile bid for J. Walter Thompson, the most famous of Madison Avenue's advertising groups, in June 1987. I had just finished my book *Managing Know-how*, and regarded the idea of hostile bids for 'people business' as the ultimate in folly. However, it wasn't as hostile a bid as it seemed because all was not well at JWT. There was considerable internecine strife, and although the board rejected the tiny WPP's impertinent $566 million offer, there were others in the organization who were more sanguine about the deal.

Sorrell also knew that although the main assets went down in the lift every evening, JWT's age and reputation also had value. He'd become a collector of people business brands, and JWT's was the strongest of them all.

Sorrell saw WPP as a purely financial brand that, unlike the Saatchi & Saatchi agency, would keep a low profile in the advertising world. The key business-winning names were those of the agencies themselves, not their owner's.

He saw his job as purely clerical: he would relieve agency leaders of the distractions of financial management, impose on them the mildest of cost disciplines, and raise margins from a little below to a little above average. That was all that was needed to ensure the acquisitions wiped their faces and created added value for WPP shareholders.

But the JWT deal showed that Sorrell is also a strategist and the possessor of acute 'entrepreneurial alertness'. He spotted the opportunity embedded in JWT's thin margins and internal squabbling, and his City skills, well honed at Saatchi's, had persuaded him that in the market for corporate control, no quoted company, however large or established, is immune from a tempting offer to investors, wherever it comes from.

Early in 1988, while visiting New York during litigation WPP mounted against defectors from JWT's Lord Geller subsidiary, Sorrell was invited to dine with Ken Roman, boss of another giant of Madison Avenue, the Ogilvy Group. They talked about cooperation in media buying, and Roman revealed that JWT and Ogilvy had been discussing the idea of a merger before WPP's bid.

Nothing came of the media buying talks, but Sorrell was very intrigued by the idea of a merger and began to explore ways in which it might be financed. The Ogilvy Group, led by flagship agency Ogilvy & Mather, would be dearer than JWT because it was more profitable, but Sorrell reckoned there was room for margin improvement and the client lists looked a good fit. Finance would be more difficult because the market remained weak after the 1987 stock market crash, but WPP had just sold JWT's Tokyo office block for £109 million, way above book value, so its balance sheet was strong.

Sorrell began buying Ogilvy shares, to just below disclosure level, in late 1988. This is a favourite raider's gambit. It reduces the effective cost of a successful bid, while at the same time locking in a dealing profit to cover costs if the bid fails. The break came when the other guy blinked.

Sorrell had been trying to win Ogilvy's agreement to a $45-a-share offer but Roman rejected it and, hoping that publicity would kill Sorrell's grandiose ambitions, he announced his rejection. Instantly, the question was not whether the Ogilvy Group would be 'taken out', but at what price and by whom. In the end Roman and his board felt the best answer was $54 a share ($864 million in all) by WPP.

But with the giant-killing over – there was nothing left to go for after Ogilvy, apart from Saatchis, and Sorrell didn't like the look of that catastrophe in the making – Lady Luck rendered her account in the form of the deepest advertising recession since World War II. WPP was better insulated than most because it had a better geographical spread of business and because below-the-line, where WPP is strong, held up better than advertising. In the end, though, WPP's heavy financing costs began to overwhelm the shrinking cash-flow and Sorrell was forced into a crisis restructuring of WPP's debt in the spring of 1991.

However, he doesn't seem like a man who has looked over the abyss and been afraid. He's relaxed about it all. He regards it as just another part of the clerical job. And unlike the much more desperate refinancing at Saatchi & Saatchi, WPP's crisis has not led to the departure of its leaders, or to the fire-sale of its business assets. Sorrell never even contemplated that. He had his two 'trophy' brands as WPP's corporate finance adviser, Bruce Wasserstein, called them, and he was going to keep them.

'We've got a marvellous business here,' Sorrell was enthusing in September 1991. 'It's very complex and it's getting more complex. You just have to sort your way through it. The core businesses are all exceedingly good.'

I asked whether the extra interest costs associated with the refinancing would constrain WPP's development from now on.

'Each business is different,' he replied with a delphic smile. 'They all need capital but the biggest part of the capital is people.'

Jenny Pitman Racing Ltd is one of the top four National Hunt training stables in the country. She won the Grand National in 1983, and has bagged two Cheltenham Gold Cups (including 1991, when her son Mark won on Garrison Savannah). **Jenny Pitman** is at the top of her unusual profession.

She described her daily routine in her autobiography. Up at 6 a.m. (except on Sundays); a cup of tea and a glance at the *Sporting Life* in bed while the lads muck out and feed the horses; older horses saddled by 7.30; a variable workout, depending on the day of the week and the age of the horses, with Pitman watching from her Shogun; the first string back by 8.45; grooming and attending to hooves until 9.30, then a big breakfast.

Breakfast is an important event. There's plenty of talk, and everyone, including the occasional owner, is there. On days when they have a runner, especially in winter when racing can start at noon, there is often a rush to get the runners packed off to the racecourse, the other horses exercised and breakfast out of the way before it is time to leave for the meeting.

'Racing people seem to spend half their lives driving to or from race meetings,' says Pitman. 'There never seems to be quite enough time, and consequently they do twice the speed of most motorists. Our mileage can be phenomenal; my Datsun, purchased in 1981, had nearly 70,000 miles on the clock before it was 18 months old.'

As Pitman explained in a radio interview in 1991, the pace hardly lets up during the relatively quiet period, between National Hunt seasons.

'There's a lot more to running this business than training the horses. Horses' records have to be got up to date, and the yard has to be disinfected and painted. I like the horses to come back into an environment that is clinically immaculate. It costs us between £12,000 and £14,000 during the summer to set up again for next season.'

The yard, with room for 80 horses, has been built up over a period of 15 years, and work on the house has only just been finished.

'I always saw the potential here,' Pitman remembers. 'When I bought the place, Tony Stratton-Smith said he thought I was very brave and very foolish, and that I would be better off in the yard with the horses than in the house.'

She employs 35–42 people, depending on the time of year. The lads get four or five weeks' holiday, the horses get 10 to 12 weeks and Pitman gets 10 days.

'I haven't a clue of turnover, but I keep a close eye on the business. I do the minimum possible long-term thinking with the business side. I stick to the training. I learned to use a calculator recently but my son Paul (the accountant) talks in metric – I have to make him convert it back, so I can see what things are costing me a ton.'

So what special quality in Pitman's operation has made it so good? One can look at her business in a number of ways. It is a bit like fund management, in that owners pay you a fee to look after their horses in the hope that they will perform better under your care and schooling. The frequency with which your horses win obviously affects the attractiveness of your yard relative to other yards, but there's more to a yard's reputation than its record at the racecourse.

'The special quality is care,' Pitman explains. 'A lot of my owners are successful business people, but when they get involved with horses, all that goes out the window and they make silly business decisions. They come round yards like they go round schools to see whether they're suitable for their children. I always ask what would I think if I walked round this one.

'My business has thrived because of my reputation. This is a good yard. I've never had a person who has been here to look over the yard and then decided to go somewhere else.'

The fact that good yards also tend to be winning yards is a consequence of their quality. Good yards attract owners, and so give the trainer a wider choice. If you run a good yard, where the horses seem to their owners to be happy, and if you have, like Pitman, enormous experience and understanding of horses, all you need is 'an eye for a horse'.

'Some say that my biggest fault is that I fall in love with my horses. I find it impossible not to. I have principles from the old school – it's my way of doing things. My family was never wealthy, but I was always taught that if a job is worth doing, it's worth doing properly. I've always designed things around the horses, although it's not considered to be cost-effective to be concerned about the mental as well as the physical attitude of the horses.'

Another feature that has helped turn Weathercock House into one of the largest yards in the country, and certainly the one with the highest quality horses, is that Pitman has never been a very expensive trainer.

'I've always been middle-of-the-road on charges. I won't put my hand too far into the sweet jar. That's not acceptable. And I've always been more interested in the quality than the quantity. Flat racing yards have a massive turnover every year. I like to keep my horses. I own Burrough Hill Lad now, and I hope Garrison Savannah will spend the rest of his life here too. They do the best they can.'

Only rarely does she buy a horse of racing age. She does not see herself as an owner, and maybe owners might suspect if she ran a string that her horses were getting preferential treatment and the pick of the jockeys.

'I bought an Irish horse once because I liked it and it was cheap. An owner called me, wanting to buy it. He said that if I liked it, he was sure it was good. I said he must come down and see it. You can't buy a pig in a bag. I sold it to him for what I paid for it.'

But though Pitman demonstrated long ago at Hinton Parva

an uncommon ability to turn weary and difficult horses into winners again, she also attributes some of her great success to good fortune. 'I've always been very lucky with my horses. I've been fair to them and treated them well, and they've rewarded me. If I had been an owner, I would have bought 98 per cent of the horses I have now.'

There's a curiously equivocal quality about the ownership of racehorses. Owners may own them, but trainers are highly possessive about them. Corbiere ('Corky' to his friends), Pitman's 1983 Grand National winner, was owned by Alan Burrough and his son Brian, but if you'd asked Corky to whom he belonged, he would probably have said Jenny Pitman or his lad, Gary.

It is unlikely that if **Chris Curry** had his time again he would do things very differently. But then it is equally unlikely that there will ever be a time quite so full of opportunities for electronics entrepreneurs as the early 1980s.

'The Acorn experience didn't change me,' he says. 'The main lesson I learned was to be more circumspect in contractual arrangements. Customers cancelled their orders but we found we couldn't cancel our orders with suppliers.

'I don't believe our product ideas were wrong, and neither do I believe we overestimated the market. We were hit by a sudden, artificial dip. But it is true product development was getting slower and slower. Software was a much bigger job than it had been a couple of years before, and the Electron was terribly slow – that was a significant contributing factor. We also had a very large research and development department, and we were probably looking at too many ideas. Management became very difficult.'

Curry's key interest was, and remains, mass market products. 'You can either compete in an existing market or you can try to create a new one, which is what I prefer, although it can be a swine to achieve.'

His main project right now is Keyline Shopping, an advanced electronic home shopping system he has designed and developed. It allows shoppers to choose goods on-screen, order them and then pay with a smartcard without getting out of their armchairs.

'There's a huge educational process, which is very difficult in a recession when people are more conservative. The chief problem with Keyline is that it's not just the terminal — it's two-ended. You've got to convince service providers, and when you've convinced them, you have to convince the public. It's a chicken and egg problem.

'It needs a lot of promotion in conjunction with the service providers (retailers mostly). It depends on the relationship between retailers and shoppers. We're just the catalyst with an enabling technology. We don't have full control.

'The potential is colossal. That's why I'm so interested. It could be much bigger than Acorn. Projected earnings in the business plan exceed the highest profitability ever achieved by Acorn in year four.'

Hardware for the system is supplied by another Curry company, General Information Systems (GIS). 'We're leaders in the development of low-cost terminals, on-line systems, communications and smartcard on-line payments systems. We already supply terminals to other companies. We don't make them ourselves; we subcontract, as ever.'

If GIS becomes a major supplier of terminals, it could grow into a company like Acorn, but Keyline is very different. 'It's a network provider,' Curry explains. 'Once it's set up, there's very little to do apart from monitoring transactions and taking a little bit of money every time. It can be very slim. It's like a royalty stream.'

GIS has also developed other products too. 'We developed a satellite receiver system long before Clive [Sinclair] or Amstrad, and we launched a home control system, using a computer that sent signals around the mains. That was a market misjudgement. We didn't realize home computers were used just for word-processing. It was before its time. The big companies are doing it now.

'So many of these markets are denied to small companies

now — you've got to be large and you have to form international alliances. The word is standards. Much as I'd like to create *de facto* standards, it doesn't happen often.'

Curry has a new software standard product on the back burner; he calls it a 'Virtual Machine'. It is a standard design for a computer that he believes could break the stranglehold on computer development exerted by the chip-maker Intel, and IBM's software supplier, Microsoft. Curry would earn profits from licences issued to hardware and software suppliers.

At the beginning of the 1980s four small UK companies, all led by entrepreneurs committed to acquisition-led growth, set out to emulate the huge success the industrial holding companies Hanson Trust and BTR had achieved in the 1970s. They were Williams Holdings, Evered Holdings, Suter and F.H. Tomkins. All were started at about the same time and they kept close company for the first few years. An early investor in Williams, in May 1984, was ECI. Although it had lagged a little in 1984–5 when the pace began to quicken, Williams made up ground by mid-1986, when each had a market value of about £150 million.

Then Williams seemed to find another gear. By early 1988 its market value was roughly the same as the market value of the other three put together, and its brand portfolio included such names as Crown and Berger paints, Polycell, Rawlplug, Swish curtain-track and Fairey bridges.

Nigel Rudd and **Brian McGowan** attribute their greater success to caution. They saw the winners of the last conglomerate building race, Hanson and BTR, both refuse to burden their balance sheets with significant amounts of debt. Although they know debt is always cheaper than equity in theory, they also know that debt increases the risk of being wrong-footed by sudden unforeseen events, like a stock market crash or a sharp rise in interest rates at a time of weakening demand.

There is a principle in the theory of conglomerates, proposed by Harvard management guru Michael Porter, among others. It says that once an acquisitive company achieves all the so-called 'added value of review' (from cutting costs and tightening operating parameters) in the businesses it buys, it should sell them. McGowan knows the theory, but says that it doesn't apply to Williams.

'I ask myself, if I was starting today, which of the large industrial holding companies would I buy? With Hanson, I would buy few of its businesses, but with Pearson's I'd buy them all. It's all to do with the quality of the businesses. If you have 80 per cent of the fire protection market for airlines, and if the chances of continued growth in air travel are high . . .'

McGowan argues that 'churning', as the buying and selling of portfolio companies is known, is probably the right strategy for Hanson, but not for Williams. 'They'll increase margins from 3 to 7 per cent because they're not class businesses. We have margins of 17 or 18 per cent because we can grow the business. But we do sell when we get irresistible offers.'

The occasional irresistible offer is actually quite useful because another Williams theme is the upgrading of the portfolio.

'Looking back five years,' McGowan mused in September 1991, 'I thought some of the businesses we had then were the bees knees. We've done a lot of upgrading since, but the process will slow now. We'll develop the businesses we have. I keep telling people that we don't need to buy anything.'

Maybe so, but barely a week after we spoke, Williams made a hostile £700 million bid for Racal Electronics, and a week later announced it was poised to buy the fire protection business of Rockwell, the California-based aerospace and electronics group.

The hostile offer for Racal came as something of a surprise because after the failure of their hostile bid for Norcros, Rudd and McGowan said they would not make another hostile bid 'because we're not good at them'.

Some people say that the problem with the industrial holding company model is that it makes companies more efficient at the expense of making them less entrepreneurial. McGowan takes issue with this as well.

'We often introduce entrepreneurial flair for the first time — we don't suppress it. If we decide to get into something completely different, we'll say we don't know anything about this business but we've got 5,000 employees who are experts.

'It's a two-stage process. When we buy a business, we send in the "hit squad" [the Williams post-acquisition team] and then we pick winners. We say, "You know where you want to go from here. What do you want to buy? Who do you fear most?"

'We combine their operating knowledge with our corporate finance skills. All our acquisitions are done that way.'

I pressed the point further and suggested this was not true entrepreneurialism; it was just infecting each new portfolio company with the Williams acquisitiveness, but McGowan would not yield.

'We do new product development too, but that doesn't hit the headlines. We bought a mad professor's invention in the fire protection area recently for £200,000. Swish (the curtain-track business) is always developing new products.'

# Reflections

Timing, luck and determination seem to be the general themes of this chapter. You have to see things early, you have to be good at what you do, you have to be stubborn, and fortune has to smile on you to start with. When the good luck comes first, the bad luck is less likely to be fatal.

Sometimes fortune picks you out, as Whittam Smith felt it had done, sometimes it comes disguised as danger, as it did with Duckworth, when defensive action to compensate for an anticipated decline in existing markets led to reluctant expansion.

Sometimes fortune deserts you, as it deserted Noble and ARV, and sometimes bad luck turns out to be good, as in Payton's case, when the collapse of Norton Warburg led to his gaining control of his company.

But an important point about luck, good or bad, is that to

have it you must be active. It's no good sitting around waiting for the lucky break. You must put yourself in the luck flow and be alert for opportunities and, above all, you have to stick with it.

An entrepreneur I know once told me that the most important quality of all is stubbornness — a refusal to give in. But stubbornness can also be dangerous, and if it is associated with the project, rather than the company, it can sometimes be fatal.

As the business careers of Richard Branson and Anita Roddick also show, doggedness must be flexible and allow you to change tack at crucial points, to abandon projects that are going wrong, and always to keep an open mind about the ways in which your skills and talents, and those of the people who work with you, can be best exploited.

# CHAPTER FOUR

# The human being

# CHAPTER FOUR

# The human being

Everyone suspects, quite rightly, that hidden within all entrepreneurs are human beings who are quite ordinary.

Entrepreneurs are different, but not that different. They are more affluent than most, and often more fulfilled, but they have similar physical and emotional needs to everyone else, and in their non-working lives they encounter the same personal problems and the same opportunities. They have rows with those close to them, they read, listen to music, watch television and worry about their health. They have friends whose company they enjoy, they have wives or partners they are emotionally dependent on and they often dote on their children. Usually, like the rest of us, they have a sense of place and of what it is to be home, and they find, as we do, particular subjects that interest them and certain pastimes they enjoy.

**Chris Curry** has two daughters, Victoria and Fuschia, six and four respectively. 'I was a late starter,' Curry explains. 'I had too much of a good time as a bachelor.'

Fuschia was named after a leading character in *Gormenghast*, Mervyn Peake's wonderful series of Gothic novels, which Curry loved. He also used to have an insatiable appetite for science fiction. Lesley, the mother of his children, was his secretary at the ill-fated Acorn during the latter stages. They are not married, but they're together. 'I'm not remotely religious,' says Curry, explaining the lack of nuptials, 'and formality irritates me. The only important thing is to behave well.'

He admits to being ambitious for his children. He would like them to be successful 'with reasonably high visibility', but he does not expect them to go into commerce. He is hoping they will be artistic but says it's too early to tell.

Curry has maintained contact with several school friends. Two are lawyers, one is in the Middle East, and a few are farmers. None of them have any connection with the electronics and computer business. He had to rediscover his non-business friends. At one time, during the early Acorn years, he had nothing but business friends. 'For a six-year period, from 1977 to 1982, I was totally committed to Acorn,' he recalls. 'There was no time to look outside.'

He has business friends, too. He is part of a network of men and women who understand electronics, computers and tele-communications, and who, in their various ways, are trying, like him, to make a living or a fortune out of it.

Curry says the main difference between his business and non-business friends is the subjects of conversation. 'When I meet business friends, all the talk is about the strains and difficulties of business. Most people in the same business are suffering seriously right now [summer 1991], and though no one really wants to see others go down, we're all hoping to hear of someone else's misfortune. There's a superstition that there's a fixed amount of good luck, and that if someone has bad luck, there's more good luck to share around the rest.'

Though there was an occasion during the desperate days for the home computer-makers in late 1984 when Clive Sinclair and Curry were reported to have come to blows at a Cambridge restaurant, the two men remain good friends.

'I meet Clive quite often. We usually discuss product ideas and have a general moan about the economy. I enjoy those talks.' He talks to his erstwhile partner, Hermann Hauser, about once a month. Hauser is another member of the network who believes in a finite amount of good luck.

Curry does not collect and has no formal hobbies, but admits, with some reluctance, to an 'interest in the world about me; animals and plants'. He would hate to be associated with the environmentalists — to be bracketed with the 'greens' and their sandals and rucksacks — but he has a deep interest in his estate, which he sees as a microcosm of the environment.

'I like finding cures for sick trees and plants, and over the years I've learned quite a bit about horticulture and silviculture.'

Curry has a strong sense of home. Apart from a brief period when he had a flat above Acorn's offices in Covent Garden, he has never lived far from Cambridge. He likes the area and seems very settled there. He enjoys the house, too, and gets involved in repairs and maintenance work.

His appetite for science fiction has faded now, and he reads little. He admits, rather shamefacedly, as if it might be a sign of age, that these days he finds himself re-reading books he has enjoyed in the past.

'I'd like to write but I don't because it requires diligence and an ordered life. I'm too interrupt-driven. I've often been criticized for being more interested in answering the phone than in getting on with the job at hand. Sometimes I fantasize about getting a disabling disease so that I can do nothing but read and write.'

He worries about his health more now. 'I'm extremely unfit, horrifically overweight. Table tennis is the only game I'm any good at and that doesn't involve much exertion. I always used to be pretty fit, up to five years ago. I keep telling myself I'll do something about it.'

At Harvard they spoke of a person's life being divided into three circles — family, business and society. **Martin Sorrell** sees his life as being focused on the first two circles. He says his social circle is very small.

He grew up in Mill Hill and then, when he left home, bought a flat behind Madame Tussaud's. It was there he met James

Gulliver soon after he had returned to the UK to work for Mark McCormack. In 1971, after his marriage to Sandra Finestone, he bought a house in Hampstead Garden Suburb where they have lived ever since.

'I don't have any consuming passions outside business and my family. I have no art collection' — a reference to Charles Saatchi's famous collection — 'and I'm not involved in any political activities. I'm not a gardener, and I don't have a large country estate, but I do enjoy cricket and skiing.' He used to be very keen on chess, but plays rarely now.

He and his wife Sandy have three sons, and when I spoke to him last summer, the eldest was about to go to university, having worked for a while with a law firm in Hong Kong. The second son has dabbled in advertising and the law, and the third, more laid back than the others ('because Sandy and I were when we had him'), is 14 and is happy to play cricket every day in the summer.

Family is very important to Sorrell. He admits that business takes precedence, but never to the exclusion of the family. 'I always try to be at home on weekends, and that's usually possible, except when I'm in the Far East. I played in the fathers' match at my son's school during both the JWT and Ogilvy deals.'

All his sons have gone to boarding school, but Sorrell has no fixed ideas about what he would like them to be. 'I want them to do what they're happy doing. They seem to be a little more professionally orientated than I was. The eldest could well end up as a lawyer.'

Sorrell would like to be for his sons what his parents were for him. 'My father was very wise; a good adviser. It's up to them. All I can do is give them a start. My parents were not wealthy, but they kept me at university for five years.' He does not subscribe to the widely held view that in these intensely competitive times it is impossible to be a successful business person and a successful family person.

'There is only a conflict,' he says, 'if you don't manage it properly. It's a problem to which you can find a solution.'

More than anyone else in our group of entrepreneurs, **Richard Noble** has dedicated his life to his dreams. Perhaps, if his second major project (described in Chapter 3) had been a success, something resembling a conventional life might have developed by now.

Although he has a good relationship with his parents, they are still bemused by the lifestyle their eldest son has chosen. 'We've lived, month by month, for 15 years,' he says. 'My parents can't understand that.'

He has two younger brothers – one a yacht broker in the south of France and the other an assistant curator of the Queen's pictures in Buckingham Palace. 'We get on tremendously well,' says Noble.

His wife, Sally, the first to sign on for the epic overland journey to South Africa, seems content. They've been married since 1979. 'She always knew about the bug,' says Noble, 'and we always agree everything together as a family. We look at each project beforehand.' Sally and their daughters, Miranda (12) and Genevieve (10), were all at the successful Black Rock Desert record attempt, and Noble was delighted by the way the two girls came to see themselves as integral parts of the team. Since then the girls have been joined by Jack, now three years old.

Having been what he calls a 'late developer' himself, Noble has no idea yet how they will turn out. 'I'm giving them the best education I can, but I'm not trying to point them in any particular direction. My father was always trying to push me into the army but I hated the idea. I'm being very cautious.'

Though Noble says he has 'an enormous number of friends', he appears to have a quiet social life (apart from the passion for cocktail parties that consumed him for a while). 'These projects are so intense, there is very little time to relax, apart from things like painting the house, or mowing the lawn, when you can let your mind run free.'

Apart from occasional trips to the theatre, Noble relaxes by reading voraciously – mostly technical books about aviation, engineering and, of course, record-breaking. 'When there's a

**99**

project on, it's complete absorption. I read everything about it to see where the others went right and where they went wrong.'

The closest **Brian McGowan** gets to heaven is when he sets out on an early spring morning in the Scottish Highlands with a rod, a picnic of smoked salmon and Dom Perignon for lunch, and the prospect of a good day's fishing.

'I spend a lot of time fishing for trout and salmon,' McGowan says. 'My biggest salmon so far was a 25-pounder.' He also plays tennis twice a week, swims quite a bit, skis and goes to Dire Straits concerts. In fact, skiing is on a par with fishing in McGowan's book because 'they both let you lose yourself, totally'. In terms of relaxation he thinks that he and Nigel Rudd, alike in so many other ways, are very different. 'Business is a vocation for him, but not for me. I do it because it pays well. When I'm not working, I've got better things to do.' These include spending time with his family at his home near Uttoxeter in Staffordshire. 'I love my house – I fiddle with it endlessly. We've got 16 acres, a bit of a lake and we breed ducks.'

He married early in 1966 and has two sons. The eldest is '20 going on eight' and has just finished five years at Wellington College. 'He wants to be a jazz blues pianist. He's talented and I indulge him outrageously.' The second is '17 going on 42' and his father has no idea what he'll be – 'a gigolo, perhaps?'.

McGowan has always been fascinated by the Rothschild family – by how great, inherited wealth enabled so many members of the dynasty to excel in so many different areas. 'There are great things you can do when the family is rich. You might be able to do something really worthwhile if you can remove the financial pressure. I might have been a great violinist or a butterfly collector if I could have been indulged by my parents. I've tried to give my children opportunities I didn't have, and a better education. The only thing they can't do, as far as I'm concerned, is nothing.'

His wife Julia appears to have accepted her husband's rapid advancement with total equanimity. 'I never had any doubts, and she had even fewer. I found the mid-thirties a bit trying — I sometimes wondered whether I'd make my deadline for being financially independent by the time I was 40. Julia would've been surprised if I hadn't.'

Work was everything to **Keith Duckworth** — hobby, vocation and the source of peak experiences. He did a little water-skiing in the early 1960s, but it wasn't until after the completion of his great masterpiece, the Ford DFV F1 engine, that he showed any signs of self-indulgence. It was a substantial sign, however — a Brantly helicopter, looking like an elongated, horizontal teardrop, which he bought in 1968. He loved it and took an impish delight in its registration number: G–AVIP (Geddit? 'Gee! A VIP!'). He would usually fly for an hour every Sunday until he was 'grounded' by his first heart attack in 1973. He still has the Brantly at his home near Northampton where he has lived for 10 years.

Home was always an extension of the workplace. 'I worked on the DFV design at home,' Duckworth recalls. 'There were no problems. My wife was amenable and my son bounced on a baby bouncer while I worked.' Seen through the eyes of the child, Roger, the scene has intriguing dramatic possibilities. What was this man, who was father, doing there so quietly, staring into space and squiggling on that big board? The answer was that he was designing what would be the most successful racing engine the world had ever seen, and is ever likely to see — a masterpiece that, in its way, was on a par with the Mona Lisa.

Duckworth feels badly let down by his body. His first heart attack, when he was 39, put paid to his flying, and a second attack, in 1987, led to bypass surgery, an abrupt end to his lifetime smoking habit, and his withdrawal from active work at Cosworth. Later he returned as a Cosworth consultant and got married again, to Gill, but he soon retreated, more or less full time, to Buckby Folly where he keeps horses.

'My stepdaughter and wife are keen on horses,' he explains. 'They are not part of my life, although I do have admiration for those who do eventing. I've always liked bold and dangerous sports. I do some now myself, on a Honda Pilot, a 400cc, 2-stroke dune buggy. I've done a few off-road races.' He appeared briefly last year on the BBC's *Top Gear* programme, enthusing about Pilot racing. He also rides a jet-ski and windsurfs at his place in Minorca which he bought eight years ago.

He has four children now: two of his own and two from Gill's first marriage. His daughter Tricia is 28 and runs a wine bar near London Bridge. His son, Roger, is a development engineer at Cosworth and a keen rally driver.

The great man still thinks a lot, sitting with paper and pencil mulling over engineering problems, and he also reads 'odd bits'. Lately, he has acquired some impressive-looking computer equipment and is trying to teach himself to use CAD (Computer Aided Design) software.

People sometimes ask **Bob Payton** why he has no interest in children. He has two answers. The first, which we shall consider later in Chapter 6, is that this is not the kind of world he'd like to bring children into, and the second is that he *is* interested in children.

'I've got 23 restaurants, two dogs, four horses and a cat. They're my surrogate children. I have a deep-seated need to create things' – witness his restaurants, a derelict school in Leicestershire which he turned into a house and the way in which he transformed Stapleford Park, Melton Mowbray, from a crumbling pile into a successful hotel, which, when I spoke to him, he had just decided to sell.

'I'm a sponge for trivial knowledge,' he says, 'and a student of contemporary culture.' He reads *Melody Maker*, the *Face* and *Cosmopolitan*, but his heart and soul are in the past. He regards himself as a sardonic neo-Victorian and says that the happiest days of his life were when he was a teenager. 'The world was never better than in 1963. I sometimes think civilization ended with "Bye Bye Miss American Pie".'

He knows all the Four Seasons' hits and he has a passion for old movies. He loves playing with his video-editing deck at

Stapleford Park. 'I've got *Casablanca* down to three minutes,' he says, 'and I'm collecting all the song and dance stuff. I used to be a dancer.'

He still fancies himself at disco-dancing. 'I asked whether I could be one of Janet Jackson's back-up dancers. I thought a white, balding 47-year-old would be good.'

Payton is a big man — 6 feet 3 inches and 18 stone — but told the *Evening Standard* last year that he sees himself 'as a 5 foot 10-inch, 13-stone, blue-eyed person'. He uses an exercise cycle from time to time, but appears unworried by health problems. 'I try and keep myself alive. I don't drink but I eat too much.'

He also hunts with the Cottesmore, which he says is 'really scary'. It's part of his love affair with England. 'I'm here because this is the past. I'm a Victorian person and Britain is neo-Victorian. I like it here. It's not as good as it was though because the countryside is under threat. Theft is on the increase.'

When I met Payton in the Chicago Pizza Pie Factory he was with his friend Fred from New York. Fred said that a lot of international people say England is the best place to live. 'It's the most civilized Western country, though it's not as civilized as it was. There's still a respect for fundamental values here. Look at Thatcher's and Major's actions during the run up to the Gulf War.'

Payton did not demur. He thinks the relaxed and easy English atmosphere he found so attractive in 1977, when he had to choose between staying in London and opening a restaurant, or going to New York to become a high-powered ad-man, is in the process of disappearing, but his roots are here now. It seems unlikely that he'll go back to the US.

**Andreas Whittam Smith** believes that those for whom the family is too important to sacrifice on the altar of work have two windows of entrepreneurial opportunity, of which he took the second. 'My children were just leaving school and going to university when I started the *Independent*. You can do it in your twenties, and then another window begins to open up in your mid-forties.

'I've had no problems with the family. They supported me to the last decimal point.'

But those 1,000 bridges he's had to cross have changed him. 'I learned to work hard. First I learned you could work twice as hard, and then three times as hard, and then four times as hard. It's changed my rhythm. Now I get up at 6.00, go running at 6.30, return, shower, dress and have breakfast at 7.45. I start work at 8.00, reading the papers and preparing for the first morning meeting. I leave home at 10.30. I usually get home at about 9.00 in the evening, but I'm out working about three nights a week.'

He listens to a lot of music and has been going through what he calls a 'Brahms season' lately. 'I may go back to it, but I suspect I will listen to more and more chamber music from now on.' He is also an avid reader of non-business books and is particularly fond of biographies. 'I've just finished an excellent biography of Wordsworth − it inspired me to read a lot of his stuff I'd never read before − and I recently read *100 Years of Solitude* [by Gabriel Garcia Marquez] for the first time. I know everyone else read it years ago.'

He also enjoyed *Indecent Exposure*, about the management at Columbia Pictures, and has been getting more interested in history. 'I've been reading about the Fourth Republic, 1945–1960. It is a part of French history I don't know enough about.'

Apart from running, which he says he's a little addicted to, he likes walking. 'Valerie [his wife] and I have a project − we're walking the length of the Thames from the barrier to the source. We've got as far as Abingdon.'

**Jenny Pitman** has managed to a much greater extent than any of the other entrepreneurs featured here to integrate the various parts of her life − business, family and social circles − into a harmonious whole.

Weathercock House is a home and a headquarters − a place for both resting and working. The administrative office is next door to the kitchen, and most of the people around her have at least two roles. Mark Pitman, winner of the Cheltenham Gold

Cup in 1991, is a beloved son, as well as one of her jockeys, and David Stait, whom she met soon after the split from Richard Pitman, is a counsellor and colleague, as well as a husband in all but name.

The horses, too, are members of the family, playing the role of beloved friends as well as profitable assets. There is no distinction between the roles, and no hint of exploitation.

'Horses have taken us over,' she grins. 'My life is totally surrounded by horses. I've always built my social life round my work. You get into trouble doing it the other way round.' She says she sometimes finds it difficult to get the right balance 'where the work can pay for the pleasure, and give you enough time to enjoy the pleasure', but when it is so hard to distinguish one from the other, that can only be a very minor problem.

She spoke of her feeling for horses in a radio interview in 1991 after Mark's Gold Cup win on Garrison Savannah. 'Horses in my life have always been a bit like people's cats and dogs. I was brought up with them. I always think that when I retire my ideal retirement home would be a nice sitting-room with probably six or eight stables round the outside, with the horses' heads looking in. And they could be all my old buddies.'

Jenny gets a little irritated when people suggest the family thing is being taken too far when she gives her son Mark the best rides. 'Last year was the first he had had a retainer from the owners. As his experience and racing increases, his position on my list of jockeys improves. Mark's ideas are the same as my ideas. If, for any reason, I didn't think he was doing his job, I'd drop him. Over the years there have been many successful parent/child relationships in National Hunt racing. It's taken as perfectly natural when it's father and son.

'Mark feels it personally. I watched him in the winners' enclosure after the Gold Cup and saw years of frustration and pain drain away from him. Part of it was putting the record straight for his father who had always come second. I saw him look up at his old man in the BBC commentary box and punch the air. There was so much joy in his face, I didn't mind, even though his father had pissed off when he was 11.'

For all her toughness and brilliance, there is something of the *grande dame* about Jenny Pitman. It is as if she has been so busy over the last 15 years becoming who she is and building up her company into one of the best of its kind in the world that modern life has been moving on without her noticing it. She knows it and it amuses her.

'I don't shop very often — I normally get the girls to do it — but David and I were in Leicester recently for my mum's funeral, and we nearly got certified at Asda. We wanted some ham and cheese, so we went to the delicatessen. Everyone was queueing at one end of a long counter. I couldn't understand it. Then I noticed they were looking at these numbers on the wall. I asked a man what they meant and he told me about how I had to take this ticket with a number on it and wait my turn. I also have problems with queueing at Marks & Spencer. The difference is, people will show you in Leicester — not down here. They're too sniffy.'

# Reflections

It may be that some entrepreneurs do live almost entirely in the business circle of the three circles of life that Martin Sorrell learned about at Harvard, and hardly at all in the family and social circles. But it is natural there should be less division than is usual in other families between business and the other sides of their lives. Business is an area in which they've excelled — it is their strong suit. It would be surprising if its influence was not palpable in other areas of their lives. After all, they and their families live within the material rewards of their enterprise and good fortune. Business has been good to all of them, and maybe they do not view hard work as the chore it sometimes seems to others.

# CHAPTER FIVE

# Stress and money

# CHAPTER FIVE

# Stress and money

This chapter was originally going to be two chapters because I believed that if there were two things that distinguish entrepreneurs from ordinary people, they would be the amount of money they have and the amount of pressure they work under.

I suppose I had a vision of the entrepreneur as being a kind of modern Damocles – living forever in the lap of luxury and forever on the edge of a nervous breakdown. But the more I spoke to those who have spared me their time, the more I became convinced of two things:

- entrepreneurs are not motivated by a desire for wealth;
- entrepreneurs rarely feel a moment of what ordinary people know as 'stress'.

Ask the next entrepreneur you meet about stress and likely as not his or her eyes will glaze over. They simply do not know what you are talking about. They frequently get into high-pressure situations, but they never find it stressful – they quite like it. In fact, some admit to being addicted to it. Most of them work better under pressure. Duckworth, for example, believes that it was the knowledge that he was about to go under that concentrated his mind and led to the storm of original thinking that produced the A2 camshaft for the Ford Formula Junior engine.

A moment's thought will reveal why this must be so. Stress immunity is a necessary quality for entrepreneurs because if they couldn't stand the heat, they would have to get out of the kitchen. It is evolution in action. Those who have stress immunity *may* succeed; those who do not have it *will* fail. Success is a sign of stress immunity, though it is hard to say whether it is genetic or the result of experience.

A thing you seldom worry about when you're rich is money. It is a general concern when you're becoming rich, but when you have arrived, you tend to have so much of it that you don't feel the need to look after it with much care.

Although **Andreas Whittam Smith** became an entrepreneur quite late in life, he says he has always had an ability to relax.

'I've been running since 1971 and that's very important – it gets a bit addictive. I also have an ability to be calm. I'm professionally calm. I abhor rows and shouting.'

He, too, repudiates the suggestion that he was motivated in any way by a desire for wealth when founding the *Independent*. And despite the arithmetic that indicates his 1.5m shares in Newspaper Publishing plc, the company that owns the *Independent*, are worth close to £4m (on the basis of the 250p a share price of the rights issue in summer 1991), he does not regard himself as a wealthy man.

'I've only ever sold 5,000 shares. I will probably sell the same amount once a year because it's tax efficient, but no more than that. Eventually, I expect I will put the shares into some sort of charitable trust.'

He took out a second mortgage to pay his share of the first fund-raising, and since the payments are quite heavy, he may sell a few more shares to reduce them. For the rest, Whittam Smith seems quite unconcerned by the financial implications of his achievement. 'Money is nice,' he says, 'but I didn't do it for that. I did it for a variety of other reasons.'

I met someone, not long ago, who is a passionate advocate of what he called 'equine therapy'. The idea is that the special relationship between horses and human beings is symbiotic in a psychological, as well as a physical, way and that people with psychological problems can sometimes be helped by introducing them to these big, gentle animals, with their distinctive personalities and their ability to inspire and, apparently to reciprocate, feelings of deep love.

If there is any truth in the theory, **Jenny Pitman** is well placed to know about it having spent her life in 'equine therapy'. More to the point perhaps is that stress seems alien to her because of the lack of conflict between her family and business lives. As revealed in the previous chapter, this is not because of the way she has reconciled them, but because of the way she has integrated them.

She is another entrepreneur for whom the word 'holiday' has a less than wholly positive meaning. 'Holidays are a bit of a pain; sitting in the sun, and being eaten by insects. I go to Jersey. I don't like sunbathing and sightseeing. I won a round-the-world trip for two to Australia once, but I didn't want to go, so I sold it to the local bobby. When I go on holiday, I pack one suitcase and I unpack it once.'

She admits to having difficulty, sometimes, in expressing her feelings. 'When Mark won the Gold Cup, my mum was there for the last time. When I knew we'd won, all I wanted was to get the important bits over with – like shaking hands with the Queen Mother – and then slope off and go to my mum. But it never happened.'

In Jenny Pitman's case, a comfortable living and a property, the value of which must run well into seven figures, is the consequence of an appetite for winning, not an appetite for money. For her, money has sometimes been a business problem – her accountant, Robin Platt, used to say, 'Let's give it another six months and see what happens' – but has rarely been seen as a spending opportunity.

In her autobiography, *Glorious Uncertainty*, she pointed out that being a top-class National Hunt trainer is not a route to great riches: 'Any idea that I may have of becoming an overnight millionairess through winning the Grand National is

**111**

a myth, and my fee from the race — approximately 10 per cent of the winning prize money — was spent mostly on celebration parties for either the owners, my family or friends, or used to continue the improvements to our home. Apart from the small items of jewellery I permitted myself, the winnings were not spent on luxuries.'

It looks as if the company will be inherited by her sons but not yet. 'I'm happy to help them,' she says, 'but I'm not happy just handing it over. Mark is a jockey, but I have two sons to consider. Paul works in accountancy, so in theory he should have a good earning power, though Mark (14 months older) is way ahead financially at the moment.

'I like to treat them equally. I bought some premium bonds for them once and one of them won £50. I split it between them.'

'I used to feel stress before I became an entrepreneur,' says **Brian McGowan**. 'But not any more.'

He points out that he and Rudd do not run the businesses in the Williams portfolio. That task has been deputed to Roger Carr. 'It's a triumvirate now. Roger is the best manager I have ever met. He runs what we buy and he has an input into the merger decisions. Our role is to act as non-executive directors who attend weekly board meetings. We're not exposed to pressure in the same way Roger is. Our job is to see where we're going next and to handle investor relations and public relations, internal and external. It is a full-time job because these things are very important.'

It was the desire for financial independence, not for money in its own right, that drove McGowan, and now he has that. Apart from fishing, skiing and his home in Uttoxeter, he seems to have few expensive tastes. Most of his wealth is tied up in his house, a comfortable flat in London near Grosvenor Square, his shares in Williams which at the last count were worth £2.9 million, not counting options, and shares in Burnfield plc, worth over £1 million, where he is non-executive chairman.

**Martin Sorrell** admits he felt 'embattled' from time to time when the WPP debt rescheduling was being put together, but never 'hassled' or 'stressed'. 'It doesn't feel like that. This is a holding company, so we are basically dealing with bad news — with the downside. I'm so used to pressure that I'd probably miss it. If it's organized, it's not stress, strain or hassle; it's life.'

He says he feels more stimulated when something very intense is going on. He enjoys it and makes full use of all the new technology. 'The cellular telephone and the portable fax have been enormously important. Together they've vastly increased the rapidity and the volume of communication. And it's going to get worse [he means, better] with videophones. The key is in managing your time and in selecting important communications. If you find it stressful, you shouldn't do it.'

He switches off when he's skiing, which he's addicted to, and when he's with his family, but he admits with only a trace of ruefulness that he doesn't like to be out of touch, even when he's on holiday. 'I ring the office every day, and I do take a phone and fax machine with me. I'd far rather know about a problem, even if I can't do anything about it. I'm incurably nosy.' And he doesn't like to be away for any length of time. 'Two weeks is too long. The last two years we've taken four-day breaks in the UK in August. That's worked well.'

He finds it hard even to conceive of a time when he is not fully occupied. 'I'll probably do it until I drop', he says.

He's not very forthcoming about his money. His shares in WPP have a market value of £700,000, but they've been a lot higher than that. He admits to being a bit of 'a hoarder', but he's lived in the same house for 20 years, and the only visible sign of unusual wealth is a flat in Switzerland which he uses on skiing trips. In sharp contrast to the company he runs, Sorrell does not appear to be personally acquisitive.

**Chris Curry** steers clear of situations he thinks he is likely to feel uncomfortable in. 'I didn't want to take instruction from someone I'd appointed myself, so, unlike Hermann, I decided to leave Acorn after the Olivetti takeover. I don't fit in to a large corporate environment.'

His partner Lesley was there during Acorn's decline, so she knew what it was like and how it affected Curry. 'I've never known anything different,' he says. 'Life has never been relaxed or without high levels of tension. I'm accustomed to it. I don't like going on holiday. It seems such a waste of time, lying around doing nothing. People say I'm addicted to stress but it doesn't feel like that.

'I find risk stimulating but a lot of people seem to be risk-averse; they require comfort or they suffer distress. My parents are like that. My father was not ambitious, except to preserve the status quo, but I couldn't live without risk.'

He thinks the best antidote to stress is achievement of some sort and he also finds it relaxing to spend some time on the estate and on garden matters.

Curry doesn't mind talking about his net worth but says it's variable. 'Most of my money is in companies. If one or two get under way . . . At the peak Acorn was worth £180 million, and I had 40 per cent. Within a year I was down to 5 per cent, and the company was worth £20 million. The shares I have now are not saleable.'

He bought Croxton Park, a fine, 18-bedroom Georgian mansion, with a 700-acre estate a few miles west of Cambridge in 1983, nine months after Acorn went public. He paid £1.6 million for it. At the last valuation it was said to be worth £3.2 million, but he has spent a lot on it.

He has bought more land since, including the hamlet of Croxton, and is now seigneur of 700 acres of arable farming land and 300 acres of parkland. He seems settled there. The 200-year-old, sparsely-furnished 'pile', as his friends call it, is crumbling a little at the edges but is structurally sound and smells comfortably of polish and age.

'I'm not a serious farmer,' Curry says. 'I don't do it for a living. You can only make a business of it if you're very large because the return on capital is minute. Farmland costs £2,000 an acre and you're lucky if you make a profit of £120 an acre. It makes a small profit, though. It pays for the gardeners.'

**Richard Noble** is another entrepreneur who has discovered the secret of managing pressure so it doesn't become stress.

'I went through it, particularly with the aircraft company [see Chapter 6], though that was a different kind of stress. You can handle pressure if you take it in stages. I rather enjoy it. I like juggling opportunities and alternatives.'

Though Noble was honoured with an OBE for bringing the Land Speed Record back to Britain, he has not made a fortune from his high-profile career. He was not motivated by money, and he thinks that if he had become wealthy, it might even have been a disadvantage. 'It's interesting, the relationship between achievement and money. If you look back, the great artists did their best work when they were highly stressed. Money can be damaging, and a lack of money can actually be beneficial. If people understand that you've got nothing, it's sometimes easier. If you're the Aga Khan [see Chapter 7], and you start off with £30 million, it's more difficult to raise more.'

And Noble thinks the disciplines of relative penury can also be useful in the areas he has chosen to work in. 'The quality and the courage of your decision-making depend, to some extent, on your personal finances. If you've got a lot of money in the bank, you tend to take the safe option. If you haven't, you've got less to lose and you're more likely to take the more challenging options. Money can often be an inverted stimulus.'

But he doesn't do it all for love. He is paid a salary when he's on a project and he also does a lot of public speaking.

He never sells himself as an OBE, though, because he thinks it lacks relevance for his project fund-raising and speaking engagements. 'I don't use it because it can set you apart.'

**Keith Duckworth** was very surprised by his heart attack in 1973, but he does not attribute it to the pressure of work.

'I didn't feel particularly stressed at the time and I don't think the heart attack had anything to do with stress. I had bad pipes, that's all. They're bypassed now.'

There was certainly pressure at work, but he developed his own way of dealing with it. 'I used to cultivate the humour of despair. You have to learn to laugh at adversity, or you end up in the nut-house. The more desperate the situation, the funnier I found it.'

But he acknowledges there are business, if not psychological, dangers associated with the fast growth Cosworth experienced from time to time. 'When people admit they're stretched, the number of mistakes rises to an unacceptable level,' he says. 'I've found to my surprise that people actually *wish* to be promoted to the level of their incompetence. I did that with myself.'

Duckworth believes he was rescued from that mistake by his great friend and ally, Alf Vickers. 'Fortunately, I managed to find in Alf Vickers a managing director of outstanding ability. He was the best bloke in the company. We met when we were both recovering from heart attacks. I thought, "This is a sharp lad", though he's older than me. Alf got us through the transition from a small to a largish company. He produced a system that allowed me to get on with my job. All I ever wanted to be was chief engineer.'

Duckworth also disproves the Kirzner idea that entrepreneurs are driven by a desire for gain. 'I've never been interested in money,' he says, 'and largely because I've never needed much, I've very rarely been short of it. I've never borrowed, except for a mortgage and small overdrafts for the company. I don't agree with borrowing. It is one of the biggest immoralities.'

When Cosworth was acquired by United Engineering Industries (UEI) in 1980 for £6.35 million — one of the bargains of a decade in which vendors usually came out in front — Duckworth held 85 per cent of the equity and so received £5.4 million before tax. He had 'The Folly' by then, and the place in Minorca, and he stayed with the company for another eight years on a good salary.

It does not take a maths degree to work out that, despite

selling his company for what now seems to be a ridiculous price — Vickers, Cosworth's present parent, paid £163 million for it in 1990 — Keith Duckworth cannot be anything other than a very wealthy man.

Stress and **Bob Payton** seem mutually exclusive phenomena. It is very hard to imagine him struggling with self-doubt, or getting himself into difficult situations he can't handle or extricate himself from. He is similar to Jenny Pitman in that the line dividing his family life from his business life is hard to define. Payton the restaurateur is virtually indistinguishable from Payton the human being. There seem to be few conflicts between the circles of his life.

His home, at the time of writing, is Stapleford Park, and he spends a lot of time relaxing and talking to friends at his various restaurants.

'For me personally,' he told Kippenberger and Burns in 1988, 'my greatest pleasure is when I walk into the Chicago Pizza Pie Factory in Paris and the place is filled with French people. Over the speakers I hear disc jockeys who were famous in Chicago when I lived there in 1967. They're playing some really good oldies all the time. So I'm listening to my favourite DJ on the radio and I turn round in the bar and there are the Chicago Bears on television and I'm in my restaurant in Paris, France. I have died and gone to heaven. For me, that's incredible.

'Then I leave Paris and go to Leicestershire where I own a 500-year-old house. I go to Stapleford and I just sit and think, "This is unbelievable, this is a dream sequence."'

It is as if his business is his solution to living in Europe in the 1990s, when his heart is in another time and another place — in the 1960s in Chicago. That such a self-indulgent re-creation of youthful innocence and hedonism should have turned out to be such a successful business formula must be a constant source of pleasure for him.

Payton seems more introspective than the other entrepreneurs in this book. There is a self-consciousness about him

— an awareness that the style and character of Bob Payton is a marketing asset that needs to be promoted. But he doesn't have to pretend. The Payton that is the spirit of the business is the real Payton. He is selling the authentic persona. He is on stage all the time, but he's not playing a part — he's entertaining people by being himself and by giving them what he likes. They can take it or leave it; mostly, they take it.

And he wasn't driven by the desire for wealth, either. 'If I'd wanted to be rich, I would have opened 75 pizza pie restaurants. Every penny I have is in the business, but I like my little trinkets.' He showed me an expensive watch and a new Japanese electronic organizer. 'I want the best of everything.' He looked up at all the Chicago memorabilia adorning the walls of the Hanover Square restaurant and waved his hand around. 'Each poster here I bought, borrowed or stole. I find things.'

# Reflections

The inescapable conclusion from the entrepreneurs' testimonies thus far is that success and the material benefits it brings tend to solve more problems than they create.

The stereotype of the neurotic entrepreneur wholly obsessed with money, careering through life, leaving a string of broken relationships in his or her wake, while lurching from one nervous breakdown to the next, is a myth. Successful entrepreneurs are, by definition, high-achievers. They have proved their point. They are relaxed and self-possessed in all kinds of company, well supplied with self-esteem and all the ones I have met have an excellent sense of humour.

It might be convenient for those who achieve less in their lives if they could believe that the price of wealth and success is always unhappiness and discontent, but it simply isn't so.

Natural selection is clearly at work here. The stereotype of the neurotic, highly-stressed entrepreneur, if it has any validity at all, can only apply to those who have yet to make it or who have failed to make it. Those who succeed are rewarded not only with wealth, but also with peace of mind. Though they often remain active and ambitious long after they have emerged above the stress zone, their achievements tend to make them fulfilled personalities. They have their monuments.

The novelist John Fowles has suggested that people are driven not so much by the desire to be somebody — the Freudian *ego* — as by the fear of being nobody — the *nemo*. Success removes that fear.

# CHAPTER SIX

# Visions, dreams and philosophies

# CHAPTER SIX

# Visions, dreams and philosophies

A quality common to many, if not most, entrepreneurs, which probably arises from the self-esteem with which their achievements endow them, is that they often hold very strong views and opinions. This applies not only to their own specialist areas, but also to broader political, economic and social issues.

However, this quality is considerably less evident among the entrepreneurial leaders of public or otherwise high-profile companies. I suspect this is not because they are any less opinionated than other entrepreneurs, but because they feel less free to express their opinions. They may take the view that their own personal reputations belong, in part, to their businesses and that it would be irresponsible to put such assets in jeopardy just for the satisfaction of letting off steam about some controversial subject.

Gerald Ratner, successful leader of the Ratners high-street jewellery chain, got into very hot water with some shareholders for unguarded comments to the Institute of Directors about the quality of the goods his shops were selling. Candid Ratner was obliged to eat his words in public, repeatedly.

But notwithstanding the natural reserve of those in high-profile positions, the views and opinions of entrepreneurs are of considerable interest because they are the product of a special kind of experience that is of great economic significance.

**Keith Duckworth** admires entrepreneurs, but he finds it hard to see himself as one.

'I see entrepreneurs as the wheelers and dealers. In Britain we recognize artistic, musical and mathematical talent, but we despise the entrepreneurial talent; the guy who swaps his "sixer" conker for something, and then swaps again and ends up, after 30 deals, with a computer or a tape-recorder. It's intuition – the ability to see value.'

He says the reason why there are so many more entrepreneurs in electronics is that all you need is a soldering iron and a few components. Barriers to entry are lower and theory is at least 'vaguely applicable'.

In mechanical engineering, on the other hand, the possession of, or, at least, access to, machine tools is a qualification criterion. You also need practical knowledge about methods, materials, heat treatment and so on. 'You require serious capital equipment right from the start because you soon find out that things aren't made very well if left to subcontractors.'

Duckworth sees himself as 'a practical fellow who got lucky' and believes that what made Cosworth financially viable was 'inherent in the way I know how many beans make five'. That meant things never got out of hand.

'My aim was not to maximize profits. That's not a reasonable brief because there are such grave differences between going for short- and long-term profits. Company chairmen are judged on a five-year stint – it's comic opera. I've never had faith in the judgement of accountants. The profit quoted is meaningless.'

And he has always been very much against what he calls 'the monkey and the jar of nuts'. He says British business people are too eager to grab, and that makes them short-termist.

'Public companies cannot afford to take a long-term view. A long-term view can only be taken by a private company, or by a nationalized industry.' He likens the short-termism and the acquisitiveness of public companies to the agricultural strategy of 'farming to leave', i.e. not maintaining assets you plan to abandon. 'It can be very profitable, and if you're not spending money on fertilizer, you've money to buy others out. It's a horrendous problem.'

But Duckworth's approval of state-owned industries because they can afford to take a longer view is not unqualified. 'You cannot afford monopolistic industries and monopolistic unions,' he insists. 'My uncle had a private haulage firm. When the industry was nationalized, he found he couldn't sack anybody because there was nowhere for them to go. Previously, they could go down the road and join another haulage firm. You have to be able to sack people, otherwise you have no control.'

Although he disagrees with conglomerates, he was attracted to the original concept of United Engineering Industries as a 'club of entrepreneurs' and he remembers it being 'quite a stimulating environment'. Generally speaking, though, he is against public quotation.

'I've got problems with the City. As far as I am concerned, the sooner someone drops a bomb on it the better. Money was designed because of the weaknesses of the barter system. It was never supposed to be a commodity in its own right. The City is totally irresponsible and totally incompetent.

'In the old days, new companies were financed by businessmen – they saw that a bloke knew what he was doing and was going to succeed. It isn't a matter of cash-flow. It is intuitive. It should be about looking at the opposition and seeing that this guy should be able to do better.'

He approved of the Business Expansion Scheme in its original incarnation as the Business Start-Up Scheme because he saw it as an attempt to reinvent the old patron/investor idea. He was disgusted when BES money started pouring into leasing schemes and property development.

Duckworth also disapproves of tax relief on mortgages, life assurance and pensions because it distorts the market and increases the amount of money in the hands of financial institutions. 'The market only works,' he argues, 'if people approach it gradually. The pension funds are too powerful and thus easily able to swing the market.'

He is equally scathing about accountants, and the role they play in mergers and acquisitions. 'Acquirers should do management audits, not financial audits – the accounts are meaningless. In many cases, those things to which you can put numbers are irrelevant.

'Look at the way power-stations got bigger and bigger, based on demand growth estimates. Each new unit increased capacity by a tenth, and yet doubling the size only added half a per cent to efficiency, which was invariably dwarfed by demand forecasting errors. It's like purchasing machine tools. The important thing isn't what it costs, but the utilization and unscheduled down time. An entrepreneur understands that and takes it all into account.'

According to Duckworth, another part of the general modern malaise is a widespread inability to sit down and think.

'I think originally and completely on any subject. I cannot help thinking and analysing. I'm very curious and curiosity drives you to learning. I look at something like that [he points to an audio system] and sit and think about what goes in, what happens when it's inside, and what comes out. I'm trying to reinvent it. I might be wrong, but then again, I might design it better.

'It is surprising how many people are surprised by things that you would expect to happen. You should never be surprised by the inevitable.'

Duckworth thinks politics are a waste of time – he seems to have almost as much contempt for Westminster as he does for the City – but he admits to an interest in public affairs.

He feels strongly, for example, about education.

'I think post-war developments in our engineering education system have been disastrous. Previously, the industry was dependent on a few theoreticians at universities, supported by people with Higher National Certificates and the student apprentices, many of whom studied at night school. So you had theoretical engineers, those with some theory and some practical experience and tradesmen. There was a nice balance of theory and practice.

'After the expansion of the universities, you no longer had that. There are too many people at university. You cannot expand universities without reducing standards. Nothing is more certain than that 80 per cent of a person's possibilities are fixed at birth. Education and environment deal with the remaining 20 per cent.

'This is fundamental. If you want a new racehorse, you breed from two good 'uns. It is true that, sometimes, two bad 'uns produce a good 'un, but when you cannot prove something, you have to look at the fundamental chances while keeping an open mind. Education just exacerbates differences that exist at birth.'

Duckworth's strikingly unfashionable views on the respective roles of nature and nurture in determining an individual's capabilities, and what seems to him to be society's adamant refusal to acknowledge the truth of these matters, have made him deeply pessimistic.

'I'm watching the end of civilization,' he declares with what might be mistaken, were it not totally out of character, for a trace of embarrassment at his own extravagance. The decline in standards that he finds so depressing is evident everywhere – in companies, the education system and in government.

'If the management of a company is to be elected by each employee having one vote, it's going to result in a badly run company. But this is the way Great Britain (and other democracies) Ltd elect their "boards of directors". As far as I can see, democracy says everyone should have a say, not that everyone should have the same say. The difference in say should reflect people's ability and how hard they work. Most people are either dim and diligent or bright and idle. The diligent and the bright should have more say than the dim and the idle. The voting system should be linked to the amount of tax a person pays – voting power should reflect contributions to government coffers and thus society.'

The enormous benefit Cosworth derived, in his view, from its ability to bring concepts close to fruition on the drawing board, thus avoiding costly trial and error with prototypes, has instilled in Duckworth a profound belief in the power of design. He also believes that concentrating effort on it can reduce cost and time of development.

'In general, elected governments have an up-and-running system for operating their countries and they only have to carry out small changes – a development exercise with which they can reasonably cope. Governments are not normally called upon to change the operating system completely, as Russia is having to do, or make a new country, as the EEC seems to be drifting towards. In both these cases, a major design exercise is required, during which all inter-related matters are considered and solutions found on paper before being implemented. Piecemeal introduction of isolated changes is disastrous, but this is what is happening in the EEC and governments don't seem even to see the problem.'

**Chris Curry** has been a member of the Conservative Party and of its social epicentre, the Carlton Club, for many years. He voted Labour in the 1973 general election because they were the only party against the Common Market, but in 1974 he stood for Parliament as a right-wing independent under the banner of the United Democratic Party on a platform that was anti-Common Market and monetarist. He may stand again, one day.

'More than ever now, I'd like to get to a steady state in my business affairs, so I could take up politics seriously. I'm furiously anti Edward Heath. I regard him as one of the great destroyers of our time.' He objects passionately to the bureaucratic procedures in Brussels and he believes with equal passion in the logic of markets.

When Maragaret Thatcher arrived, it seemed to Curry for a while as if monetarist dreams had been realized, but later he thinks she lost her way.

When he was younger he avidly consumed the ideas of Milton Friedman and the great Austrian economist, Friedrich Hayek, through the pamphlets published by the Institute of Economic Affairs (IEA), the so-called 'right-wing think-tank'.

He was also very impressed by a book called *Must History Repeat Itself?* by Anthony Fisher, an early IEA luminary, which was a cogent free-market attack on the Common Market.

'I rang him when I was preparing my manifesto in 1974,' Curry recalls. 'He said two things: "Go to the IEA library" and "It's not worth going into politics; politicians are just vehicles. It is better to join ginger groups and exert influence from the outside."'

Curry thinks that may have been true at the time. Certainly the IEA itself was very influential, but things have changed now. 'It was different in the days of the intellectual politician, when the Fabians and the Monday Club were strong, but from Thatcher onwards politicians have become immune to outside influence.'

Other books that influenced him were *Half Marx* by Tufton Beamish, and *Still to Decide*, Enoch Powell's anti-Common Market polemic.

Curry regards himself as quite close to being an anarchist, and feels particularly strongly about what he calls 'the three "rotten boroughs" of politics': the legal profession, the party system and the education system, which he believes should be 'completely ripped apart'.

He believes the British are 'still capable of creating more things than most', but that they suffer from an 'impossible' economic environment. 'It's not about taxation. That's OK now. It's an attitude to long-term investment in industry that stems from short-term City greed and short-term political expediency. British companies didn't grow, so they bought things instead. They've been denied to us as vehicles for improvement. It would change instantly if the economic conditions changed – if the true entrepreneurial spirit was set free.

'We need to get rid of market distortions in crucial areas – subsidized mortgages and tax relief on savings, for example. The latest round of inflation was caused by house prices. If it goes much further, Britain will have no say at all – the world will be run by German and Japanese industrial systems. Most of Australia is already owned by Japan.'

But Curry thinks the basic system here is probably right. He feels uncomfortable with the US corporate culture, which is too 'domineering', but likes America's free-wheeling society. If he had to choose, he would much prefer a free society to a free corporate culture.

The Acorn experience notwithstanding, Curry is still driven by his dreams. 'I like to do things before anybody else – that's much more difficult now. There were wonderful opportunities 20 years ago. I'm all for the future. I've got to be because I have high aspirations. I have to get even. I feel no resentment about Acorn; I still see it as a very much under-valued, but I've got to get back – to leave a monument. I don't know why. I'm not egotistical. But it would be nice to leave a monument. It's pretty horrible to be a nobody and I don't like being yesterday's man.'

Contact with the wealthy comes with the territory of being the top National Hunt trainer. Prime horseflesh is an expensive commodity and only very high net worth individuals can afford to hire the training services of **Jenny Pitman.**

But for all this close association with wealth and privilege, little of the politics of élitism appears to have rubbed off on her. 'I don't like to see people going hungry, or getting ill and not being treated. I want things to be better and for there to be fewer disasters and catastrophes. I suppose I'm basically Conservative, although I don't like the way they talk to people, with plums in their mouths. I'm opposed to the Labour Party telling me what I should do with my money; not letting me send my kids to private school, for example. I'm still paying taxes, after all.' And she has no brief for trades unions.

'I remember going to a meeting where they were talking about a strike. I was one of the few who voted against it. I can't believe you can't talk to one another.'

Though she is far from being a political animal, Pitman has no particular dislike of politicians. 'I'm a strong admirer of Margaret Thatcher – particularly of her stamina and never being ruffled. When she resigned, it was the first time I'd seen her at a loss. Then Kinnock went for her and she switched to automatic pilot.

'I saw her at an evening do once. She gave an off-the-cuff speech — it was brilliant. She only showed her feelings and personality occasionally when she was in front of cameras. There was a bit of show-biz about her — an incredible lady.

'I think John Major's beginning to get his act together, but I sometimes wonder what effect it's having on him and his family.'

Pitman pays into private health-care schemes for herself and senior members of her staff, but not because it's a nice perk. 'I don't want to queue-jump, but I can't afford to be off sick and I can't afford for them to be off sick either. I tell them, "I'm not being generous; it's because I want you back at work."'

Like most entrepreneurs, Pitman doesn't suffer fools gladly, and she can get irritated by officialdom and compromise. 'Certain situations crop up in our job — people read books about them so they think they know, but they really know bugger all. There are some very good people at the top of our business, but I've always tended to see things in black and white, not shades of grey. I'm not a fence-sitter.

'When you're so sure of things, there can be problems, like when I was doing repairs to the house and I felt someone had screwed me. I paid more to a solicitor than I saved because it was a matter of principle. I reckoned after that he wouldn't try to pull that one on me again, and he might not try it on other people less able to protect themselves either.'

Pitman is a great advocate of straight dealing in business. 'I say to owners, "I can't promise you a winner, but I can promise you a fair deal."' But she, too, appears to harbour a fundamentally pessimistic view of life, and she shares Bob Payton's belief that the best times are over.

'When I was younger, I thought most people were okay. Nowadays there seem to be more and more people trying to screw you. It was better in our parents' day. They were an unbelievable generation. Germany was very unlucky that it tried to beat us when they were around.'

Her own personal ambitions? 'This is it,' she said. 'It won't get any bigger.' I thought, I've heard that before.

Entrepreneur!

Despite the undeniable improvements over the last decade or so in the British climate for entrepreneurs, **Richard Noble** believes several deep-rooted institutional and attitudinal problems are still inhibiting the development of a vigorous spirit of British enterprise. He says he found the problems that he experienced in getting financial help from the Department of Trade and Industry for the ARV project particularly vexing.

'I'd been talking to the DTI for several months,' he recalls, 'and had always been led to believe that they would help, but we got nothing. It seemed to us the DTI would take forever to consider our proposals and that the answer would be a predictable "No". I never knew whether they had the budget and we soon learned not to waste valuable time in that direction.

'The DTI has lost its sense of identity. The civil servants are trying to understand entrepreneurs, but they can't because what entrepreneurs do is totally alien to them. What ministers should do is put entrepreneurs into the DTI and pay them by results.'

Noble believes that his experience with officials at the Civil Aviation Authority, when he was struggling to get an airworthiness certificate for the ARV Super 2, is indicative of the same negativity throughout British officialdom. 'It tells you something about the country. New products are welcomed in other countries. Here, everyone's always very suspicious because the entrepreneurial spirit has become confused with Thatcherism and greed. The fundamental problem is that the system doesn't support the entrepreneur.'

He has become so disenchanted with the short-sightedness of the British system that he sometimes thinks the only way to get a long-term project to fruition in the UK is for it to go through a series of liquidations so that it can be funded by a number of different sets of shareholders.

But despite the bad taste the ARV experience has left in his mouth, it is clear that Noble met some 'good blokes', as he puts it, during his close encounters with the UK venture capital fraternity. Halfway through the ARV saga he remembers being invited to a conference about entrepreneurs by the head of the venture capital division of one of the banks that had

132

backed him. The plan was to subject a group of entrepreneurs and a group of bankers to a series of personality tests and then to compare the results to see if there were any significant contrasts.

'He came to me and said, "We know venture capital is about entrepreneurs, so that means that after due diligence it's all about backing horses. We want to analyse entrepreneurs to see if we can improve the odds. Will you help?"

'There was a crisis at ARV, so I couldn't make it until the second day. When I arrived on Sunday morning I parked my Montego next to rows of Porsches.

'The results of the study were the opposite of what had been expected. Entrepreneurs emerged as very steady, reliable, trustworthy, risk-averse people. Bankers were the opposite. I suggested that when we (entrepreneurs) come to see you (bankers) we come as a team who've thought about the project for months and worked out all the angles. You come as individuals and you can't be specialists in all the functions, so after the meeting, you have to go away and make a subjective decision. It's very risky for you, but not for us.'

Several months afterwards, while Noble was licking his ARV wounds, he had a talk with Adrian Hamilton (son of Duncan Hamilton, the racing driver) about the Hales Trophy, donated in 1935 by the Midlands MP Harold Keates Hales for the fastest surface crossing of the Atlantic between Ambrose Channel Light (New York) and Bishop Rock (Isles of Scilly).

Ted Toleman and Richard Branson had nearly brought the record back in 1985, when they sank 138 miles from Bishop Rock, while on schedule to exceed the 35.59 knots record set in 1952 by the liner *United States*. The following year, Branson tried again, in *Virgin Atlantic Challenger II*, achieving a crossing speed of 36.62 knots. However, the reformed Hales Trophy Committee decided not to give the record to Branson because he had refuelled on the way. In June 1990, the *Hoverspeed SeaCat Great Britain* raised the record to 36.89 knots, the fastest, unrefuelled crossing so far.

For Richard Noble 'worthwhile challenges', preferably

linked with the word 'unlimited', are meat and drink. It seemed the perfect antidote for the disappointments and frustrations of ARV. Anything could win the title, as long as it was a ship and as long as it didn't refuel. How could he resist it?

He became project director of the Atlantic Sprinter project, and he and Hamilton assembled an impressive team, including Ted Toleman as first officer, Commander Dai Morgan, RN, as captain and Robin Knox-Johnston, CBE, as tactical navigator.

The Aga Khan's announcement that he would make an attempt on the record in 1992, in a huge 70-metre ship named *Destriero*, and would immediately transit to the Olympic Games in Barcelona set the scene for a truly epic trans-Atlantic race.

An added attraction for Noble, if any were needed, was that it was perfectly in tune with the traditions of the old-time record-breakers, like John Cobb and the Campbells, to go for both land and water records.

'We pretty soon realized that conventional boat design was going to result in a conventional performance. There had been little advance in high-speed hull-form design for years and therefore we had to create the technology.

'The key to the hull-shape was the realization that because the Atlantic was unlikely to be calm, we needed a hull-form which would give us a low-drag rise in waves compared with the conventional forms which generate very high-drag increase in waves — the one aspect that is hindering the acceptance of high-speed ferries. After months of research we teamed up with military hydrodynamicist Erbil Serter and worked up his original concepts at the HSVA tank in Hamburg. When the institute's management started to get excited about the results, I knew we had what we needed.

'We tried to start building in summer 1990,' Noble continued. 'We got the construction hull up, but then the recession hit and people stopped spending money. One US sponsor defaulted on £200,000. In January we made a payment to creditors and then we found out how to do it — we developed a totally unique promotion system. Key sponsors came in, including a sponsor with 100 tonnes of special aluminium extrusion. That was a terrific milestone.'

But when I spoke to Noble in September 1991, the project was within an ace of being abandoned. Two key sponsorship deals had failed and it was essential to place an order for the hull within weeks if the *Atlantic Sprinter* was to be ready for the July–August 1992 'window'.

'It's a brilliant project,' says Noble, 'but because of the failure of these crucial deals we have lost our chance to race the Aga Khan in 1922. His boat is reputed to be costing $40 million. It displaces 1,250 tonnes, is 230 feet long, has 54,000 horsepower, needs 750 tonnes of fuel to make it across the Atlantic and will average 50 knots.

'Ours will cost another £4 million to complete and run, displaces 350 tonnes, has 33,000 horsepower, needs 250 tonnes of fuel and will average 60–65 knots. It is also very stable. We wanted to race the Aga Khan head to head. The danger is that projects like this begin to smell if they hang around too long.'

But they may well go ahead with a Blue Riband record attempt in 1993 to pluck the Hales Trophy from the Aga Khan (if he makes it in 1992, that is). Noble is restructuring the marketing side and it looks quite promising, despite the loss of the additional excitement of the race. You probably wouldn't have seen much of it on the TV coverage anyway if the *Atlantic Sprinter* goes as fast as Noble hopes.

Even if they don't make it for 1993, Noble is still young and seems far too full of passions and enthusiasms to lack a 'worthwhile challenge' for very long.

'I never look beyond the current project. The intensity is too great. You have to concentrate on one project. It's a matter of working your way through the system and of finding out how to break the system. And you have to be very sure it's what you want to do.'

It should not be in the least surprising that the politics of **Brian McGowan**, whose career as an entrepreneur began at the dawn of the Thatcher era, 'err to the right', as he puts it. 'I'm right wing economically but much more liberal in social things. I think it's disgraceful you have to wait five years for a hip replacement.'

Though McGowan is not one of those who like getting involved in causes, his experience, achievements and his underlying free-market philosophy have made him opinionated, despite the fact that his position as the joint leader of one of the UK's largest industrial holding companies demands, for the sake of his shareholders, a certain professional reticence.

He has reservations, for example, about the way in which the Tory privatization programme has been conducted. He thinks it's 'difficult to privatize a monopoly', and he has grave doubts about the quality of management at some of the large, neo-private organizations that have suddenly appeared to compete with Williams Holdings for a place in the ranks of Britain's biggest companies.

'It's okay in principle for the leaders of newly privatized companies to be paid £160,000 a year; their companies are certainly big enough. But I cannot help thinking that if they were prepared to do the same job for £60,000 a year previously, they're probably the wrong people. They haven't been through a system of natural selection.'

McGowan believes strongly, as do other leaders of industrial holding companies, in a Darwinian model of business, where the fit survive and the weaker corporate brethren go to the wall. It's the existence of this weakness within the population of companies that is the primary *raison d'être* of groups like Williams. They prey on it. They buy companies when they are weak and then make them strong, thus creating value for their own shareholders.

I asked McGowan whether he thought that when companies like his and Lord Hanson's had been around for a while, there might come a time when the disciplines they had exerted on the corporate population at large would eliminate all weakness and so break the food-chain on which Williams-type companies depend. He smiled, and shook his head.

'Businesses have life-cycles. There will always be some that are getting old and tired. There is no chance that the fuel supply will dry up because of human nature.'

He is comfortable in this tough corporate jungle and he sees Williams, with its ability to challenge incumbent management and, if necessary, to dismiss it, as an agent of the process of evolution that is improving the British corporate breed.

'To get more efficient managers, you have to have the threat of dismissal. You have to be able to say, "You're doing a bad job. Go." If they say it to me, I'll walk. When you live by the sword, you must be prepared to die by it.'

The self-styled founder of Britain's 'street-food culture' was alone in our group of eight entrepreneurs in unhesitatingly owning up to being an entrepreneur. The others all felt the term had to be modified a little to accommodate them, but it is clear that **Bob Payton** has always seen himself that way. His prominence in the media suggests that for others, too, he fits the common perception of what an entrepreneur should be like.

'An entrepreneur,' says this exemplary member of the species, 'is someone who is prepared to back his hunches with his money or his life. The crucial thing is passion. You have to be prepared to kill for it. I didn't do it to get rich. All I wanted was to open the best restaurant in the world; to do something unique. I'm an innovator, not a game player. I'm not competing with anyone else; I'm competing with myself.'

He believes that his peculiar ability, which has produced a score or more of highly successful restaurants since 1977, comes from the clarity of his cultural vision. 'I'm a student of contemporary culture in the broadest sense. I see it; I know what is happening and I know how to make it happen. I like inventing new things. It is someone else's job to take them on from there.

'I could do another six or seven concept restaurants here in London. Cloning is too easy. The challenge, for me, is whether I can do another one that's as good as the last one. I ask myself, "How have I changed for myself lately?" I do things because it amuses me.'

## Entrepreneur!

But Payton's irrepressible self-confidence and his optimism about his personal business future are mixed with a profound pessimism about the world in general. 'It's not the sort of world I'd like to bring children into,' he says, though he is hopeful that 'our generation may just escape the holocaust.' He thinks the cultural deterioration shows up in popular music. 'Compare the innocence of rock and roll,' says the man who believes civilization came to end with Don Maclean's 'American Pie', 'with the aggression of modern rap music.'

As we have seen, it was Payton's love of this lost innocence that attracted him to the 'museum' that we call England, but he fears that, here too, bad times are crowding in. 'Look at the football violence. You're making do with second best here. There's evidence of increasing wealth, but London is filthy. Someone has to have responsibility for what goes on in this town. If there's no mayor, who can we get at?

'Why are the landed gentry so shabby, and why is there this fashion of faded English elegance? Americans have much more national pride. The English only show it once a year, at the last night of the Proms.'

But Payton approved of the Thatcher era, and understands it. 'Thatcher is a neo-Victorian. England became like it was 100 years ago. The retailers have done that. Thatcher understood that people want to be told what to do. That's what happens in my restaurants — customers are told what's good. Thatcher was very good at that but I also think there's some merit in Major's classlessness.'

Payton is not specific about his own dreams but he says he's got many more things to do. 'My goal is to die penniless, but it is important to get the timing right. There's no one I want to leave it to [his wife, Wendy, is already well provided for]. I would like my epitaph to read "At least he got it all in". I'm not saving up for anything. This is it.'

One of the interesting things about **Andreas Whittam Smith** as the passionate and dramatically successful entrepreneur is that this side of his persona seems completely at ease with his persona as the sober and objective financial journalist. It is as if he sees himself as an interesting phenomenon in a world where he has been a professional observer rather than an active participant for most of his working life.

'I like the old meaning of the word "entrepreneur",' he says. 'Someone who acts as the intermediary between the factors of production. Out of that comes a business.'

He believes the environment for entrepreneurs in the UK has improved enormously in recent years. 'For 20 years I didn't use the term venture capital. Now we take it for granted. You can do it now. Entrepreneurs were not City people, so they couldn't use the City. They didn't know about it. It's much better now.'

But having seen, as a journalist, innumerable entrepreneurs rise and fall, Whittam Smith is managing his own adventure with considerable care. 'Entrepreneurs make mistakes when they take themselves more seriously. I'm in favour of not thinking about one's self – not noticing the publicity. Someone gave me some very wise advice about personal publicity – "Never inhale". If people say you're this or that, whether it's nice or nasty, try to take no notice.'

He tries to keep as low a profile as he can. Occasionally he feels obliged to play the ambassador and make public appearances for the sake of the newspaper, but he keeps such barnstorming to a minimum, and one gets the impression that he doesn't enjoy it much.

'There's a terrible danger when people think they've got the magic touch. You'll notice this office is smaller than those of most of my colleagues.'

But his distaste for the show-biz of entrepreneurial success notwithstanding, Whittam Smith remains a seriously ambitious man and appears to have a much clearer idea than any of the other entrepreneurs featured in this book of where he is going.

'I know exactly what I'm trying to do. I'm trying to build a newspaper publishing company with the same quality as the companies I most admire, like Morgan Guaranty, Mars and

Marks & Spencer. The question is, can you so construct it that it never falls below a certain high level? I've no idea whether I will be able to do it.'

Having assembled, almost single-handed in the space of just a few years, the world's largest marketing services group, it would be hard for **Martin Sorrell** to repudiate a belief in free markets. His politics were 'left of centre' when he was at Cambridge, but they have probably shifted to the right a bit since then.

He is not stridently opinionated about matters political or economic. For one thing, it wouldn't suit his style, and for another, he has shareholders to think about. But he does have strong views on the quality, or rather the lack of it, of business education in Britain.

'I wrote an article about graduate recruitment years ago and talked about the lack of links here between education and business. It's very different in America. Harvard was formed and funded by business. The British universities were mostly formed by the monarchy, government or the Church, so they're like the Civil Service.

'The pattern is established in America. At Harvard, 88 per cent of the funding comes from non-state sources, but here the business schools are only just beginning to depend more on private sources. People are still asking how far should they go? At Harvard, the professors are encouraged to take non-executive directorships. It's still quite rare here.'

He thinks some of the continental business schools are much better than the UK's in this respect. He points out that in Germany industry routinely buys equipment and software from the universities and says the IESE business school in Barcelona, with which he has links, is a good example of how religious origins need be no barrier to the establishment of strong links with industry.

Sorrell also believes the quality of the teaching in foreign business schools is higher than in Britain. 'The personalities of the professors were very influential at Harvard. I remember

Walter Salmon particularly. He was known as the "Red Baron" and was very tough and disciplined. There were some great teachers there. Here they're not so common because there's more emphasis on research.'

Sorrell does more than just talk about the problem. He is a trustee of the Cambridge University Foundation, and in 1990 he became involved with the Judge Institute, which plans to set up a management studies school in Cambridge.

The Judge Institute, as its name implies, was financed by an £8 million donation from Paul Judge, a fellow Cambridge graduate. Judge deserves at least a passing mention in any book about successful British entrepreneurs because he is said to have made more money from venture capital than any other Briton. In 1986 he took out a £90,000 second mortgage on his house to help finance the highly-leveraged £97 million management buy-out of the Cadbury-Schweppes food business. Judge wanted to take Premier Brands, as the Smash, Marvel and Typhoo Tea company was christened following the MBO, to the stock market, but was outvoted by his fellow directors when Hillsdown Holdings bid for the company in 1989. Judge netted £45 million.

Sorrell is unlikely to match that, but he's doing all right. Looking back, the one thing he regrets about his education was not spending a couple of years in industry before going to Harvard.

# Reflections

Looking back over this chapter on visions and dreams I find the longest sections are those relating to entrepreneurs who are less than 100 per cent active. Either they have retired, or they are in some way or another between projects. Part of the reason may be the one discussed at the beginning of this chapter − entrepreneurs in active life, and with a corporate reputation and outside shareholders to consider, feel constrained and so less inclined to be outspoken about their personal views.

But it also suggests that entrepreneurs have a tendency to switch between active and passive modes, and that during the latter they are more contemplative than during the former. It seems to be a matter of taking stock — of entrepreneurs using 'down time' as an opportunity to digest the experience of the immediate past and incorporate the implications in their world view. It may also be something to do with the fact that active entrepreneurs are busy people and so have less time to indulge in navel contemplation.

This spasmodic entrepreneurial pattern of contemplation and reflection contrasts with the more gradual accumulation of a world view by non-entrepreneurs, whose lives and careers are less punctuated by periodic discontinuities.

It is not at all surprising that most of these entrepreneurs have political views that 'err to the right', as McGowan puts it. The political right in Britain has been more favourably disposed towards entrepreneurs than has the left, so it would be odd if this was not reflected in their politics.

For myself, the most surprising result of this investigation into the thoughts of entrepreneurs is the deep underlying pessimism it has revealed. It is not shared by all of them, of course, and the sample is small, but it is common enough to be remarkable. I find it surprising because it seems to me that optimism is a necessary, though obviously not a sufficient, condition for the successful entrepreneur. It is hard to see how pessimism can generate entrepreneurial activity. If you believe things are more likely to turn out badly than to turn out well, how can you find the will to take risks and try something new?

The paradox is resolved when one makes a distinction between the personal and the general outlook. Entrepreneurs may need to be optimistic about their own careers, but this does not require them to take an equally rosy view of the world at large. It is obviously possible for an individual and his or her company to do well, while the world is going down the tubes.

# CHAPTER 7

# Leadership

# CHAPTER 7

# Leadership

It goes without saying that most successful entrepreneurs are able leaders. They cannot succeed without the help of others, and they cannot procure that help without inspiring in their colleagues and collaborators an unusual degree of commitment and loyalty. Either with the strength of their personality or with the grandeur of their dreams they must persuade others to follow them.

However, it is also true that while entrepreneurs are good at starting companies, they are often not so good at running them once the organizations are established. This chapter aims to look at the issues raised by this anomaly.

In the first place, the assertion that entrepreneurs often lack managerial ability in what might be called 'conditions of maturity' (either of the market they may have helped to create, or of the company itself) begs the question of whether there are differences between the management skills needed at different stages of a company's development.

Secondly, it begs the question of whether there is something about the management skills needed in the early stages of a company's development that conflicts with those needed later on. In other words, is there something about entrepreneurs that makes them less able than average to lead larger and more mature organizations?

The answer to the first question must be a qualified 'yes' — there can be differences in the management skills needed at different stages of corporate development, but it is easy to imagine situations where entrepreneurial management skills remain necessary in conditions of maturity. In consultancy companies, for example, and in other project-based enterprises, there is a constant need for innovation and an inspirational style of leadership. The business idea in such companies is intrinsically entrepreneurial. Maturity is a brief, unsustainable period preceding death.

The distinction between companies where maturity is healthy and companies where maturity is a symptom of illness is similar to the distinction between 'hunting' companies and 'farming' companies. The former make their living by going and getting, while the latter subsist by husbanding what they already have. It follows from this that in the case of hunting companies, entrepreneurial leadership is not only not in conflict with the managerial needs of the company as it grows, but it actually remains a necessary condition for development. Even in very large companies, there is much talk these days of the need to cultivate the 'entrepreneurial spirit' and, therefore, of the need for entrepreneurial leadership.

As markets become more globalized and more competitive, the weaknesses of the pure farming strategy become increasingly apparent. Good husbandry of established franchises remains crucial, but these days few large companies are content to rest on their laurels. Since no franchises are immune to attack, no companies can afford to be without a significant hunting capability.

As the cases of Martin Sorrell and Brian McGowan show, the entrepreneurial spirit remains central to the business idea of the conglomerate. Companies pursuing a 'portfolio strategy' must be led by an entrepreneurial individual or team. Without entrepreneurial alertness and the will to act, they cannot spot, and then take, the acquisition and divestment opportunities that are their *raison d'être*. Indeed, the top leadership teams of the large conglomerates, like Hanson, BTR, Williams and WPP, are probably the closest the business world gets to pure hunting organizations.

But although the need for hunting and an entrepreneurial style of leadership are becoming more widespread throughout the corporate size-range, the question of whether successful human hunters always make good farmers remains open.

**Jenny Pitman** has no fashionable egalitarian ideas about the role of a leader, and there appears to be little in the way of power politics and in-fighting at Weathercock House. 'Everyone is equal, but if there's not a leader, it doesn't work. I've got king pins − the head lad, David and other smaller wheels − but there has to be someone to tee it off.'

Her authority is even-handed and impartial, even with kin. 'Today Mark had ridden a particularly difficult horse. He had said it needed more training at breakfast, and then he said it again in the tack room in front of people. I said, "Look, when I want people to tell me about my horses I'll ask them!" I had to put him in his place when he said it in front of people. He'd already said it at breakfast.

'I try to put myself in their position. They seem to find it difficult to put themselves in my position.'

In view of the importance of love in Jenny Pitman's life and career − love for people and love for horses − it is something of a puzzle that she should have done so well in what seems, to the outsider, to be the rough and tumble of National Hunt racing. She explained the paradox in a radio interview.

'People have said to me that I'm a survivor; that I'm very tough − "the formidable Mrs Pitman". They compare me to the Iron Lady. But we're exactly the same as other people; we just have an exterior with which we cover up our feelings because otherwise we wouldn't survive. When I get my cloak and binoculars to go racing, I have an invisible armour that also comes with them.'

And she believes that National Hunt is not really as tough as people think, or, at any rate, not as brutal. 'It's a bit like a rugby match, rather than a cricket match. National Hunt races are tough, but after Mark had won the Gold Cup this year, he pulls up and the French jockey pulls up [Mark Pitman won the race by three inches] and they shake hands before they know who's won. They always do that, but you never see it in flat races.

'It's partly a sense of relief that they've both finished – there's a bond between the jockeys. National Hunt is a lot more dangerous for jockeys than the flat.'

Underpinning Jenny Pitman's leadership style is an enormous self-confidence. She understands horses because she's lived with them all her life, and she knows the National Hunt game inside out. 'Because I've worked in all the aspects of racing – starting off as a stable girl, marrying a jockey, being a trainer and now being the mother of a jockey – I've always seen the job from a lot of angles. I reckon I've got as good a view as anybody as to whether it was the jockey's fault, the horse's, or something I shouldn't have done that day.'

**Martin Sorrell** does not fit the popular model of a charismatic leader, far less the popular conception of the charismatic head of an advertising agency. In this respect he would never claim to be in the same league as David Ogilvy, for example, the founder of Ogilvy & Mather, whose initial response to WPP's bid for his agency was to call its leader 'an odious little jerk'. But the fact that Sorrell understood the feelings that gave rise to Ogilvy's outburst and that he bore no ill will towards the man says something about his powers of empathy.

Notwithstanding the aggression with which he has pursued his portfolio strategy in marketing services, Sorrell, in common with other leaders of holding companies, is an extremely charming man. He is an intellectual, but he is not one of those 'intellectual thugs', who like to beat others about the head with their brilliance. He is soft-spoken, interested in what others think and is an excellent listener.

Even David Ogilvy, he of the 'odious little jerk' outburst, owns to Sorrell's charm. In a radio interview a year later, by which time he was chairman of WPP, he publicly recanted. 'When I met him, I was bowled over. You know, he is one of those very rare businessmen who ask few questions and listen very carefully to your answers, which is almost unique. He's got a sense of humour, which is almost unknown among businessmen. He's a charming man. He's very impressive.'

Sorrell suggests there are three kinds of entrepreneur: the pure entrepreneur, the 'entrepreneurial manager' and his own kind, the 'managerial entrepreneur'. His successful career as the last suggests the secret lies not so much in the inspirational energy and vision usually associated with an entrepreneurial leadership style, as in systems.

'If you identify a growth business,' he told me in 1989, just after WPP's acquisition of Ogilvy & Mather, 'you should be able to do better than average with the right people and the right brands.' When WPP bought J. Walter Thompson and then O&M, Sorrell was brand collecting in the same way as Williams Holdings has been brand collecting. Sorrell felt that strong brands more or less ran themselves, insofar as entrepreneurial leadership is concerned, but that they were often badly managed in an operational sense.

His contribution to the positive sum game was to install management systems that would allow inspirational leaders, like Ogilvy, to get on with doing what they were good at. 'Everything we have done has been aimed at moving the two companies towards achieving average margins. The targets are not strenuous.'

He emphasized that the systems were not control systems, but monitoring systems. 'You hope to catch trouble just before it happens, or as it happens. Financial management is not the most important thing. Management's job is to enable staff to concentrate 100 per cent on client business. We separate the two. Managing the business is secondary to managing the client.'

As Sorrell sees it, managerial entrepreneurs are not so much leaders as enablers – the people who look after the boring bits, allowing the inspired and talented the space they need to exploit their abilities to the full. But there is a little more to it than that.

**149**

Sorrell also plays one of the leadership roles identified in the debate about corporate leadership that began a few years ago – that of 'coach'.

The team Sorrel coaches is not all of WPP, but those who run its business units. From his vantage point at the top of WPP, and armed with his 'entrepreneurial alertness', Sorrell is better placed than his business unit leaders to detect and understand the main developmental themes at work in the fast-changing marketing services industry. He can therefore act as an invaluable source of advice for those running WPP's businesses. This counsellor role, like a Mafia godfather's *consigliere*, is important because one of the problems with being an entrepreneurial leader is that it can get quite lonely at the top. There is often no one to talk to about strategic matters. A well-informed leader's leader, who doesn't interfere but is always available for a chat, can make the job a lot easier.

In many ways, the role of leader at Williams Holdings is similar to the role of leader at WPP. There is a system involved that looks after the day-day-day leadership, and there is a head office to which business unit leaders can go for help and advice. They are also encouraged to suggest to the top team ideas for tactical acquisitions.

The Williams leadership is a rare example of a triumvirate, consisting of Nigel Rudd and **Brian McGowan** running strategy, and Roger Carr, who sorts out the businesses after they've been bought and then acts as chief executive of operations. But Rudd and McGowan, who argue that the difference between Williams and the industrial holding groups of the 1970s is that Williams runs the businesses it buys, are conscious of a formal responsibility for their portfolio companies.

'We look after internal as well as external public relations – we make a point of visiting the operating units from time to time, for example. Someone called these occasions "Royal visits" and that conveys their purpose quite well. Weinstock [Lord Weinstock of GEC] and White [Lord White of Hanson] never meet the guys who run their businesses – that can't be right.

'Some of them run very big businesses, with £100 million or more of turnover. If you run a business of that size and someone asks you at the golf club, "What's Nigel Rudd like?", you'll feel silly saying you've never met the guy.'

Rudd and McGowan also recognize they have a leadership role among people who are not their employees. During takeover bids, for example, the Williams team works closely with the group's brokers and investment bankers. A bid is a project which needs to be managed, and Rudd and McGowan seem to be rather good at that, even when the bid fails, as in the case of the abortive offer for Norcros.

'We were at BZW's office at Ebbgate House in the City, when we heard we'd just lost the Norcros bid,' McGowan remembers. 'It was 2.30 and when the announcement came our advisers thought it was a disaster. Someone asked what we were going to do now. I said, "Open a bottle of champagne." A market-maker looked in at 6.00 and saw 40 people getting merry. He was amazed. He said, "I thought you'd lost!"

'We needed that because you have to pick everyone up. Later we had the head office in and we told them we'd succeeded in not paying too much.'

McGowan believes that when you're doing an acquisition it is important never to forget that you are playing a game − not a game in the sense that what you're doing is frivolous in any way, but in the sense that there is nothing of life or death about it. If you lose, it's not the end of the world.

'It is no different from playing a game of cricket. You have to be in it to win, but at the end, if you fail, you shake hands and say okay, who am I playing next? After we lost the Norcros bid, we sent the other side a bottle of champagne with our congratulations, but we never got a response. It wasn't a game to them.'

McGowan argues that if you adopt an acquisition-led strategy like Williams, the leadership has to take it very seriously. 'We [he and Rudd] handle the big strategic moves, like Yale & Valor [or Racal, though that bid hadn't been made when I spoke to McGowan]. You can't be acquisitive if you've got a full-time job elsewhere. That's why so many acquisitions fail. People don't feel comfortable doing nothing, but you've got to be content doing nothing for quite a lot of the time in the acquisition game.'

Karl Erik Sveiby and I in our book *Managing Know-how* (Bloomsbury, 1987), suggested that the most traumatic conceivable event for a know-how company like Cosworth Engineering is the departure of its founder. We argued that it is the company's condition at the point of the founder's departure that will determine whether it grows up and becomes what we call a 'professional organization' or whether it enters a period of terminal decline. One of the implications of this is that the leader of such a company has an overriding responsibility to make himself, or herself, dispensable.

**Keith Duckworth** seemed interested in the argument, but he was not wholly persuaded by it. 'As far as I can see, if a company is going to survive the departure of the founder, it has to find a way whereby someone of the abilities of the original person is kept in the company and carries on running it. The company is bound to change when the founder leaves, but it still needs someone with talent, competence and ability to lead it. If it's technology-based and has a 'beat-the-world' culture, it needs someone like that and they're rare and very difficult to recognize. And even after you recognize one, you have to get everyone else to recognize him too. It's comic opera.

'The circumstances have to be produced to keep that bloke, and if there are others who object and leave, the company collapses anyway. Maybe the best way is to set the successor up in a parallel organization and then bring him back in.'

Duckworth believes that all companies have a life-cycle: they are born, mature, grow old and die. He sees nothing terribly wrong in a company dying after its founder leaves; indeed, it may be the best thing for it.

'I only want to be a member of the team when I'm the leader,' Duckworth says, but he acknowledges he had a 'fairly good' team, and he admits to being 'proud of the fact that so many people stayed — like Mike [Costin] and Ben [Rood]'.

And Duckworth's doubts about Cosworth's continued commitment to excellence notwithstanding, it seemed, when I visited the company's two sites, to have retained much of the Duckworth spirit three years after his departure. And that is a not inconsiderable legacy, for it was Duckworth's personality, as much as his enormous ability, that made the company such a Mecca for talented engineers.

'After I had decided I would paddle my own canoe, I was only interested in things where I could see a logical connection between A and B. Very early on we started asking the experts why? Cosworth's culture was why? We're known for asking why?

'Why? questions need knowledge and intelligence to answer. Our culture was straightforward and honest. People knew it was better to say you don't know. In large companies people start spieling; they practise the art of equivocation.

'You've got to have a thinking system, otherwise there is a great gap. I think, "This bloke isn't thinking", so I say, "Bollocks!" People don't like it, but even bright people talk bullshit half the time; 90 per cent is average. I can't stand people talking bollocks. It restricts you and prevents you from being exceptional.'

But the Duckworth legacy to Cosworth is more than a healthy intellectual arrogance. He also imbued the company's culture with a strong commitment to neat and elegant design, and to a supremely practical approach to engineering. Cosworth, as a result, is unusual in the automotive engineering industry for the efforts it makes to get things right first time. To Duckworth, the principle seems blindingly obvious.

'There's no point in designing something bright unless you can make it well enough to demonstrate it.'

It is sometimes suggested by those who have a vested interest in deterring others from trying to break the mould of newspaper publishing, as **Andreas Whittam Smith** has done, that the problem with editorially-driven projects is that journalists know nothing about management. But this is nonsense.

Over many decades newspaper publishing has evolved a dual leadership system, involving publisher and editor. All the evidence suggests that for most of the post-war period the editors have been doing a better job at managing their side of the business than the publishers have at managing theirs.

As we have seen, part of Whittam Smith's inspiration was his frustration with the poor quality of publisher management at the *Daily Telegraph*. Borrowing a term from Chapter 2, it helped to provide 'background plausibility' for his venture – the competition simply didn't look very impressive. And as Whittam Smith points out, there is nothing radically new about the editorially-driven newspaper project.

'All the major newspaper groups were started like this – by people like the Rothermeres and the Berrys. They were people with something to say, and they also had to manage.

'The *Independent* is editorially driven, but an editorially driven paper that's run by someone who thinks he understands business *should* be very profitable. I'm still fundamentally a financial journalist. I'm an observer of business. You get a sort of feel as a financial journalist.'

Whittam Smith also believes that the insatiable curiosity of journalists, and the need of the financial journalist to understand such complicated organizations as companies, have helped him to develop a holistic view of newspapers.

'Financial journalists have honed the finding-out skill to a very high degree. I've always had a nose for it and I've never been frightened of going to the top. It takes you into all aspects – advertising, production and finance.'

He says leadership is 'the most difficult thing of all', but he thinks the combination of the publisher and editor roles has had certain advantages. He believes, for example, that cost-cutting – that familiar publisher versus editor battleground – may have been easier at the '*Indie*' than elsewhere during the recession because of the combined leadership. 'Some of the financial things others will take from me which they might not take from anyone else.'

But when I spoke to Whittam Smith in September 1991, just as the second rights issue was being put to bed, he had reached the conclusion that he could not combine the roles of editor and managing director for much longer. And he was in no doubt which of the two roles he preferred.

'My problem is that I'm not a journalist any more. I'm not doing enough with the editorial. We're going to have to change the management structure. I shall have to stop doing all the jobs that I'm doing now and spend more time on the editorial function.'

It is sometimes hard to decide the extent to which the style and the mannerisms of a foreigner reflect the foreignness and the extent to which they reflect the personality.

**Bob Payton** is unmistakably American, but is he also unmistakably Payton — or do most Americans with a fondness for Chicago, and a background in advertising, come over with the same brusque self-assertion?

People say he's rough, but his friend Terry Holmes, managing director of Cunard Hotels, says Payton's really a softie and that people mistake his honesty for aggression.

'I first met him at a seminar,' said Holmes. 'He gave us all shit about the hotel business, but he was just being honest. People left in droves and at the end there was one person clapping — me. I suppose that's the problem with us English — we lack the stomach for American-style honesty.'

But we don't lack the stomach for American-style street food and Payton has profited from that. It's not hard to see why he is so good at it either.

'I start off honest,' says Payton. 'What you see is what you get. I don't have time to mess around. I'm always prepared to talk to anyone for 30 seconds. [He says he would make allowances for a genius with a stammer.] It's not rudeness. I'm just giving them the short course.'

Payton says he's not the best manager of people but he does all right. His staff seem to like him, and the record shows staff turnover in his restaurants is well below the industry average.

'My greatest asset is a happy staff,' he says. 'But it's not easy to work here. You have to get with the programme or go. If you're not with the programme, you'll be miserable anyway. You can't let them beat you. They've got to respect you.'

He regards himself as an ideas person and dislikes managing things long-term. 'I like concentrating on things; on making them right. I did everything here. The quickest way to lay a table is to have forks in one hand and knives in another. I wrote that into a manual and trained the bus-boys and the waitresses.

'I'm patient to start with but if they're not doing it right in three months I blow up. It has to be right. When it comes to attention to detail, I'm second to none. I know that what I'm good at, I'm very good at. I get others to do the rest.'

The self-confidence is more than an act. Payton regards himself as an exceptional marketing man rather than a restaurateur and, one has to say, all the evidence suggests he's right.

'I get more letters asking for jobs from American kids than from British kids. They don't seem to want to work in a small organization.' But with 23 restaurants now, it's not that small – plenty big enough for young people to make a career in.

'It's a continual challenge,' says Payton. 'There's a lot of creativity in the job and young people move up through the organization. My most successful young manager started as a car jockey; now he's running Meat Packers in Paris.'

Apart from his ideas (he went to a de Bono seminar while at J. Walter Thompson, and sees himself as a lateral thinker), his professionalism and his attention to detail, it seems to me Payton's most powerful leadership asset is also his most powerful business asset – his ability to create an enjoyable atmosphere.

'My fundamental credo is to have a good time,' he says. 'That same spirit is everywhere in the organization – that same personality. That's why we got American football over here. I wanted to fill Wembley stadium with 70,000 people to have a good time. It's part of contemporary culture.'

At a seminar for receptionists at his Stapleford Park hotel someone said, 'We're selling memories.' Payton liked that. 'I want people to ask themselves, "Did I have a good time?" and to remember that, "Yes, I did."'

One of the problems for **Richard Noble**, when he embarked on his attempt to break the Land Speed Record, was that there were no blueprints, technical or managerial.

'The first thing I learned was that there were no precedents to learn from. Donald Campbell's British technology ran out of steam at 418 mph, so there had to be a step change. And he was funded largely by BP, so he didn't have to go out and market the project. We found it's all about teamwork – the sponsor's team and the operational team. All information was shared. The sponsors knew everything. It worked very well – they became involved.'

An example of how crucial sponsor involvement could be, came when an oil company withdrew its support at the last minute. 'Initial Services saved the thing,' Noble recalls. 'When we ran into massive cash-flow problems, they agreed to double up.' In recognition of this gesture, Initial Services (part of the BET industrial services group) earned pride of place for its initials on Thrust 2's twin tail-fins.

Noble admits he made managerial mistakes with the Thrust 2 project, particularly in the early days when they were first running on the Bonneville Salt Flats.

'Initially, when running for the record, the operational structure was wrong. It had taken so much effort to get to Bonneville that we hadn't paid enough attention to operational structure. I found that the general management and driving roles were incompatible – so much so that it was a relief to get into the car. In practice, the driver has to be subordinate to the technical director.

'At John Ackroyd's suggestion we asked Ken Norris to manage the team during the record attempts. He was very good at it; so good that we asked Ken to chair the sponsor's team meetings too. It is hard to exaggerate the contribution his unflustered and sympathetic style made to the success of the project.'

The beauty of a project like the Thrust 2 record attempt is that it has a very clear goal that can be (and in this case, was) achieved by a small number of dedicated people within a finite amount of time.

'The key to success with the Land Speed Record,' Noble says, 'was that it was a small team. The main people were there from the beginning; we learned the rules together. Problems arise when you hire people who don't share those attitudes. As you get further down the line, the entrepreneurial spirit decays and gets diluted.'

He learned other leadership lessons at ARV, too. 'As a project advances and grows, the pressures at the top make it very difficult to maintain the entrepreneurial spirit further down the line. Yet, on reflection, this is a critical requirement and we should have given it greater priority.'

Looking back, he thinks things worked pretty well at ARV in the early days and he admits he was 'happier at that stage'. Of his experience of running a company rather than a record attempt, he says, 'I felt I'd failed because we were never profitable. So far I have not found the opportunity to try another, but we'll see.'

It is clear from the history of Acorn Computers that, for a while at any rate, **Chris Curry** and Hermann Hauser were an extremely successful leadership pair. Whatever one thinks of the manner of Acorn's decline, the record shows that their partnership took the company from start-up in 1978 to the status of a medium-sized, quoted electronics company, with a market capitalization of £180 million, in the summer of 1984.

Curry's and Hauser's qualities and experiences proved to be very complementary. Curry's peripatetic progress through the hi-tech hinterland, culminating in his time with Clive (now Sir Clive) Sinclair, enhanced his basically entrepreneurial outlook with practical skills in project management and low-cost mail-order marketing.

Hauser contributed a more academic approach and a high-quality network consisting of many of the brightest computer brains at Cambridge University. The links between Acorn and the university's computer department were crucial to the company's success, and were managed by Hauser and Curry with great skill.

Acorn remains a classic example of the so-called 'Cambridge Phenomenon' – the extravagantly fruitful relationship that still exists today between Cambridge University and hundreds of small, hi-tech companies that are constantly sprouting up in the Cambridge area.

Interestingly, most of Curry's present colleagues in his various business ventures are people who came with him from Acorn, which suggests that his leadership failings were not the main cause of Acorn's demise. But he admits that by the mid-1980s he and Hauser had begun to find the leadership role quite tricky.

'Management became increasingly difficult. It is hard to set realistic development time-scales in the software area, partly because the technical problems themselves are genuinely difficult, but also because project and people management became harder. When demand for software engineers is high, they tend to become prima donnas. There is a lot more realism now.'

Looking back, Curry also thinks it may have been a mistake to take Acorn public. 'Unless the company has to be public, I would avoid it. It created more problems than it solved at Acorn. The share price was too important – the morale response when it fell was very serious.

'I would be very dubious about floating again. We talked to 3i about taking Acorn private at one stage, but if you've got external investors they need an exit. In future I want to earn my rewards from running a profitable company, not from selling it.'

The Acorn experience has also caused him to wonder a bit about corporate structures. 'I like the idea of the distributed company consisting of individuals working from wherever it suits them, within a community which may or may not be a company.'

# Reflections

The single most important theme to emerge from this chapter is that the key role of leadership is the creation of the right atmosphere.

The entrepreneurs interviewed, some of whom have serious flaws as leaders (by the standards of modern leadership theory), have succeeded because they have all managed to instil in their colleagues and employees not only the desire to win, but also a belief in their ability to do so. Part of this stems from the cultivation of a corporate arrogance that denigrates the quality of the competition and makes winning seem more probable, but it also seems to have quite a bit to do with systems.

I don't mean financial or management control systems, although they are important. It is more a matter of embedding in the corporate culture a few simple principles or ideas that everyone understands and agrees to, which differentiates the company's culture from that of its rivals. Sometimes, this systems approach to management is adopted deliberately, as in the cases of Sorrell and McGowan, but more often it is the unconscious absorption by the culture of elements of the leader's personality.

The cases where this process seems to have been particularly important are those of Keith Duckworth, Bob Payton, Andreas Whittam Smith and Jenny Pitman. It will be very interesting to see what happens to the four companies they have built when they retire or withdraw. The experiment is well under way at Cosworth already, but it is still anyone's guess whether the 'Keithless' Cosworth will succeed in its efforts to regain the ascendancy in Formula 1 racing that it enjoyed with the Duckworth-designed DFV. My impression is that there's still quite a lot of Duckworth embedded in the Cosworth culture, whatever Duckworth himself might think, and Dr Peter Nevitt, Cosworth's new chairman, seems to value that legacy very highly.

Jenny Pitman's company shares with Cosworth Engineering

the advantage of operating in an intensely competitive field, where there is never any debate about what winning means. As Pitman-trained horses enter the starting gates on race day, Cosworth-powered racing-cars roll on to the starting grid. In each case the outcome of the subsequent explosion of energy will show how well the company has been managed during the days, months and years leading up to that point.

Racing is the essence of competition, particularly of time-based competition, and leaders of organizations dedicated to racing benefit from the disciplines it imposes. The highs team members get from winning are addictive, and the lows of losing also concentrate the mind and harden the will to win next time. Such sharply focused cultures can give to a company the momentum it will need when it has to survive the trauma of losing its leader.

Bob Payton does not appear to be all that interested in the 'succession problem', but his company is probably a lot less vulnerable to the threat of losing him than it might seem. This is because he's been so assiduous in embedding himself and his foibles (he says you can never know what the crucial things are, so you have to get everything right) in the My Kinda corporate culture.

'Paytonism' has been institutionalized and has acquired a momentum of its own, capable of surviving without him. No one else could have invented Paytonism, but new leaders can see that it works and can try to preserve it.

Whittam Smith has succeeded by refining existing systems, not by inventing new ones, but it comes to the same thing. The *Independent* was a terribly exciting idea for journalists and, despite the inevitable suggestions that five years on it is showing signs of reverting to type in the way Orwell described in *Animal Farm*, it remains a powerful symbol of journalism's victory over the bandits.

It is probably easier to turn a new quality newspaper into an institution than a racing stables or a restaurant chain, but it seems to me that Whittam Smith has got closer than any of the other leaders we have considered to discharging his responsibility to make himself dispensable.

# Conclusion

# Conclusion

The previous chapters have, I hope, conveyed a little of the flavour of what it is to be an entrepreneur. This 'qualitative' research we have done into the lives of our sample of eight entrepreneurs, coupled with additional evidence from biographies and other previous work, allows us to say a number of things about the nature and origins of the entrepreneurial quality, about the extent to which its manifestations can be subdivided into various types and about some of its main features.

## Nature and origins

Let's suppose that the word 'entrepreneur' means someone who undertakes projects involving money and non-entrepreneurs, and let us also suppose the difference between these two personality types is real and not purely random. What can be said about the distribution of this entrepreneurial quality in the population at large?

There is much debate these days, as the countries of Eastern Europe struggle to forge capitalist economies from the scrap

**165**

metal of their failed centralism, about how widespread the entrepreneurial quality is in the general population. Does the potential to become an entrepreneur lie within everyone, or is it a relatively rare quality? Are there circumstances of upbringing and early life which will always cause the latent potential to emerge, or is there a genetic requirement, or a crucial confluence of associated qualities, without which the entrepreneur will be stillborn?

Unfortunately, in view of the enormous economic significance of these questions, no clear answers are available. My own view is that elements of the entrepreneurial quality exist to a greater or lesser extent, if not in everyone, at least within a much larger proportion of the population than that indicated by the number of visibly active entrepreneurs.

Sometimes the entrepreneurial quality is near the surface and becomes apparent quite quickly, as seems to have been the case with Branson, Curry and Duckworth. In other cases, the quality is buried more deeply and seems to be triggered later in life by particular and unlikely sets of circumstances. Whittam Smith, Sorrell and Noble are examples of the entrepreneurial quality in 'lurker' mode.

In many, if not most, cases it may never be triggered at all and may remain latent throughout an individual's life as a mere possibility. Circumstances are often crucial. Just as the seeds of plants need water and fertile soil if they are to germinate, so the entrepreneurial quality sometimes needs the right combination of external conditions if it is to emerge from its latent state.

All government can do to encourage what are probably large, but certainly incalculable, national reserves of latent entrepreneurialism to become active is to foster what I have called 'background plausibility'. And there are no secrets here. The effective entrepreneurial fertilizers are all well known: deregulation, tough anti-trust institutions, low rates of tax, the minimum of red tape, the removal of distortions in the savings market (such as tax concessions on mortgages and pensions), and the eradication in public procurement of all official prejudice in favour of large, established firms. For the rest, it is up to society to provide the climate and up to the entrepreneurs to fly the kites.

## Entrepreneurial types

To my mind the people we call entrepreneurs can be subdivided into four basic types.

**Game-players** These are similar to what Martin Sorrell calls 'entrepreneurial managers' and 'managerial entrepreneurs'. They see and understand the games being played in their own areas, and derive the background plausibility for their entry into the game from their assessment of the skills, or lack of them, of other players. City craft and 'financial engineering' skills are valuable assets here.

Such people are not so much creative, although there may be considerable creativity in the design of the systems and principles on which the game-playing strategy is based, as perceptive. Game-playing entrepreneurs see that there is value to be unlocked in market imperfections, that there are weaknesses in the way others are exploiting the imperfections, and that it should be possible to create value by playing a better game than average. The game-players can often be the builders of quite sizeable companies, as indicated by the careers to date of Martin Sorrell and Brian McGowan. Sorrell points out that two of his role models, Gulliver and Smilow, both built and ran businesses of considerable scale.

**Iconoclasts** These are the classic entrepreneurs – those with the vision to penetrate the future. They are the creators and the innovators, society's main source of new products, services, systems or management styles. They are thinkers with an appetite for action. They are not so much competing as experimenting with their ideas. Often they are driven by an urge to be first rather than to be best.

The attrition rate among iconoclasts is high because their visions of a glorious future often obscure the problems that lie

**167**

just in front of them. They are prone to disappearing into the 'black holes' of cash-flow crises, but sometimes they return stronger and wiser, and make it the second time.

Curry and Payton are examples of iconoclastic entrepreneurs; both have been driven by an urge to challenge the orthodoxy and the conventional wisdoms.

**Preservers** These are the men and women who refuse to accept the disagreeable decisions of others – leaders of management buy-outs, for example, when the alternative is closure, and those, like Whittam Smith, who see things are going wrong in their career areas and decide that the only way to reverse the trend is to go out and show how things should be done. They might be called the 'reluctant entrepreneurs', who would have been content to remain on the non-entrepreneurial side of the threshold if circumstances and the actions of others had not convinced them that becoming an entrepreneur was the least unattractive of the options facing them.

However, preservers are also opportunists. They require Kirzner's 'entrepreneurial alertness'. They have to be predisposed to see the entrepreneurial option.

**Enthusiasts** These are the 'accidental' entrepreneurs – those who turn their enthusiasms into careers because nothing else is so interesting, and find after a while that they are running successful businesses. Duckworth and Pitman are examples of this, and so is Noble, despite the fate of ARV. There is also something of the enthusiast entrepreneur in Payton.

It is often said that you should not confuse your hobbies and your business and it is true that there is ample evidence that successful business people seem to lose their judgement when they get involved with horses and football. But there is a lot to be said for turning enthusiasms into business interests. You tend to be more committed, you are often more energetic and, most important of all, you are obsessed with detail and quality. There seems to be no point in doing it if you don't do it right.

None of these categories is mutually exclusive. It is clear, for example, that there is a bit of the game-player in every entrepreneur, and game-players would not succeed if there was not a bit of the iconoclast in them. The preservers also need to be innovative, as well as opportunist, if they are to preserve effectively. The categories are not so much types, as qualities that are mixed in different proportions.

# General characteristics

So, granted that there are many varieties of entrepreneur, what are the common themes? What are the qualities they all have that make them different?

It may have something to do with the person's view of the world, particularly with his or her view of how mutable things are. Most people grow up with the belief that the world is more or less fixed — that freedom of movement is constrained within a fairly rigid framework. Entrepreneurs do not seem to feel that to the same extent as other people. They may be very conventional and conservative in most aspects of their lives, but there is an area — one which they feel is their own — in which everything is possible. They refuse to take things for granted.

Another common quality is a disposition to be active. Most people are resigned to the constraints of the world they find themselves in. They swim with the tide and are never tempted to struggle against it towards a different kind of existence.

A third common quality is an ability to focus great energy on a project or a business idea.

Courage is a fourth common component of the entrepreneurial character. Sometimes it is an individual's courage, but often it is a courage that comes from partnership, such as McGowan and Rudd, Duckworth and Costin, Curry and Hauser and, to a lesser extent, Whittam Smith, Symonds and Glover.

But entrepreneurial courage should not be confused with the gambler's courage. Reckless entrepreneurs rarely succeed. Entrepreneurs take risks, but they are calculated ones and do not feel as bold or foolhardy to them as they do to others who lack the entrepreneur's self-confidence and self-esteem.

There is also 'entrepreneurial optimism'. Entrepreneurs are emboldened to act by background plausibility in the first place, and in the second place by their own judgement that there is a high probability of success. They see success as more likely than failure.

Finally, there is luck. An entrepreneur is a human machine equipped with all these qualities and programmed to take a not-quite-random walk through life. If good luck comes first and there is not too much bad luck, the road that lies beyond the threshold, and that is always under construction, will lead on to fortune.

# Index

# Index

# Entrepreneur!